Futile Observations of a Blue-Eyed Ojibway: Funny You Don't Look Like One, #4

Drew Hayden Taylor

Theytus Books Ltd.
Penticton, BC

Library and Archives Canada Cataloguing in Publication

Taylor, Drew Hayden, 1962-
    Futile observations of a blue-eyed Ojibway : funny, you don't look
like one #4 / Drew Hayden Taylor.

ISBN 1-894778-16-2

    1. Indians of North America--Canada--Humor. I. Title. II. Title:
Funny, you don't look like one #4.

PS8589.A885F88 2004   C814'.54   C2004-904441-9

Editorial: Karen W. Olson
Cover Photograph: Thomas King
Layout: Leanne Flett Kruger
Proofing: Chick Gabriel and Harvey McGillivary

*We acknowledge the financial support of the Government of Canada through the
Book Publishing Industry Development Program (BPIDP) for our publishing activities.*

*We acknowledge the support of the Canada Council for the Arts, the Department of
Canadian Heritage and the British Columbia Arts Council.*

Futile Observations of a Blue-Eyed Ojibway: Funny You Don't Look Like One, #4

TABLE OF CONTENTS

INTRODUCTION

Here we are again –this time with *Funny 4*. I'm older and hopefully, a little wiser. I have more experiences under my expanding belt since the first volume of *Funny, you don't look like one* came out in 1996. During that intervening time, my subtitles have gone from mere *"observations"* to *"futile observations"*. I wonder if perhaps I've become more cynical in recent years; or resigned is a better word.

The number one thing I have learned to accept is that tragically I am not as funny a guy as I once thought I was. I don't think I'm funnier than anybody else you might come across. Instead, I have come to the realization that the Creator has a fabulous sense of humour. I am sure of it. In fact, I think my only true talent, or blessing if you will, is that I recognize this humorous trait and have trained myself to see and appreciate it.

I will give you an example. Some time ago, I was lecturing at a University of Alberta commencement. I did my usual routine and later as I was packing up my things I glanced down at the table in front of the lecturing stage. On it were a number of flyers, brochures, and various photocopied pieces of paper. One was an invitation to a barbecue. It was the beginning of the year and all sorts of social events were planned and orchestrated to get students familiar with the campus and to meet their fellow students. I looked closer, and noted that the barbecue was being held by the department of Veterinarian and Animal Sciences. I couldn't help wondering, "Do I want to go to a barbecue held by a group of vets?" Would the menu consist of leftover parts from class? That situation had the fingerprints of the Creator all over it.

I find stuff like this really funny; and occurring too frequently, to be coincidental. Like I said, I think somebody up there has a funny bone the size of a galaxy. Very few of the things I write about, are made up. I just report what I see and what I experience. It's a lot easier and cost effective. Any old-timer or real storyteller will tell you that the really funny and interesting stories are the ones that happen to your neighbour down the road, or to your great aunt, or because of the White guy who showed up on the Reserve one day. Those ones will really get you laughing.

So, here for your enjoyment, is the most recent collection of articles, essays, thoughts, ideas, and rants that I am privileged to write. Some have appeared in many fine periodicals ranging from

Windspeaker, to *The Peterborough Examiner*, to Toronto's *Now Magazine*, to more eclectic venues like Aboriginal Peoples Television Network's (APTN) *Buffalo Tracks* and CBC Radio. All of it is true (except for the parts that aren't). Hopefully, there's stuff here that will tickle your funny-bone, make you sad, make you angry, and perhaps make you think "I spent almost $20 on this!"

Welcome to *Funny 4*. (Why do I suddenly feel like a Rocky or Star Trek movie?)

AN INDIAN BY ANY OTHER NAME, WOULD STILL SMELL AS SWEET

FROM THE PEN INTERNATIONAL CONFERENCE ON INDIGENOUS LANGUAGES IN MEXICO CITY

Ahneen. That is how we say hello in my mother's tongue. My name is Drew Hayden Taylor and I do not speak my mother's language. She and I are Ojibway. We refer to ourselves as Annishnawbe, or simply translated, the People. We are members of one of the largest Nations in Canada, centered in the province of Ontario. Although she speaks English, my mother's first language is Ojibway; she thinks and dreams in Ojibway. On the other hand, I represent a growing population of Native people in Canada and the world, who belong to a first generation that do not speak our ancient language. I am told that, when I was younger, I was almost fluent; that I straddled the English/Ojibway linguistic fence somewhat more comfortably. I wish I could remember those years.

That was then. This is now. With fourteen years of education in English, add to that the influence of television, radio and other forms of English based media, I cannot converse with my mother the way she could with hers. I have tried to learn Ojibway again with little success. In Canada, more money is spent on teaching French, another foreign tongue, to people like me than our own language. This is of great sadness to me. Even sadder, I am not alone. Entire generations of Native people are alienated from their parent's and grandparent's method of communication.

At time of contact, there were approximately fifty or more separate languages and dialects spoken in the country known as Canada. Haida, Cree, Innu, Salish, Cayuga, Blackfoot, Tlingit, Sarcee, Dene', Shuswap, Mi'kmaq, to name just a few –all with a language as distinct as Chinese, German, Arabic or Finnish. A poll done several years ago in Canada predicted that within the next twenty or so years, only three Aboriginal languages will be spoken with any confidence –Cree, Ojibway and Inuktituk.

And to add insult to injury, I am a writer. A teller of stories. A contemporary storyteller who writes tales about his own people, in English. Occasionally I throw some Ojibway into the tale; but, in order to do that effectively I must contact an Aunt back home for assistance in translating or consult a local Ojibway language instructor. On a personal level, I find it embarrassing having to do this but I have no choice. Practically all my work deals with documenting, as best as I can, the humour, the drama, the essence of being Native in Canada. I am a playwright, a journalist, a filmmaker, a humourist and a few other things to boot. Yet, for obvious reasons, something is missing when I write about my people –the language from which these stories sprang. I mourn that.

There is a saying I once saw on a button pinned to a jean jacket years ago. It said, "The voice of the Land is In our Language." I believe that. We sprang from the land and the language sprang from us. So what I offer as an Aboriginal writer (who writes in English) is a filtered perspective. It's like asking a person in another room to describe a painting to you. Based on the description, you try to imagine it then describe that mental image to yet another person. It's an interpretation of an interpretation. Still, the writing is my interpretation and I guess that's better than no interpretation at all.

I'm managing to do my bit towards the cause of Indigenous language survival. Not that long ago, I wrote a half-hour television show for Canadian television called *The Strange Case of Bunny Weequod* completely in the Ojibway language. And it was a contemporary story too! A story that could have happened yesterday, written about a small Ojibway Reserve called Curve Lake, located two hours northeast of Toronto in mind. The irony being that I contacted Isadore Toulouse, a fabulous Ojibway language expert, to translate my English text into Ojibway.

I noted that Ojibway is inherently a longer language than English. What was as a twenty-six page script ballooned to forty-two pages. The Ojibway are a verbally verbose people. Needless to say some heavy editing was necessary.

When it aired on television, several Ojibway speakers told me that what was coming from the mouths of the two Cree leads (who had learned it phonetically) wasn't the Ojibway of my community, but a dialect called Odawa from Isadore's home community, several hundred miles away. I was somewhat embarrassed. All things considered, my mother understood the show and I managed to get the Ojibway language, in whatever dialect, broadcast on Canada's national broadcasting network. Every journey begins with a single step.

In Canada, I can proudly say there is a television channel devoted

11

specifically to Aboriginal programming called the Aboriginal People's Television Network, commonly referred to as APTN. There is programming from the far North in Inuktituk and lots of regional shows highlighting local people and languages. It is a wonderful move forward in the preservation of Indigenous languages. However, by far, the dominate language heard on APTN is English. It is the common language for most First Nations in Canada. As well, Aboriginal theatre plays, songs, poems, and literature are also mostly in English. Perhaps James Joyce said it best when he commented, "I am forced to write in a conqueror's tongue." I too am forced to write in a conqueror's tongue. It's the only tongue I command, and it's the only tongue that will sell in today's writer's market.

For the most part though, I can listen in my mother's tongue, and understand. I retain those abilities to some degree; but, I suffer for what I've heard wonderfully referred to as the Dog Syndrome. It goes something like this:

> You have a dog. You tell that dog to roll over. It hears you and understands what you are saying and does what you tell it to do. But the dog cannot respond the way it heard the command. My mother tells me in Ojibway to turn the kettle on... I hear her say the words. I understand the words. I turn the kettle on. But I cannot respond in the way I understood it. The Dog Syndrome. A far too common affliction in many cultures with their own language. Dog, by the way, is *nemush* in Ojibway.

I come from a country whose place names ring with Aboriginal origins. Canada is often considered to be an Indigenous word meaning "a small village or group of huts." Ontario is an Iroquoian term meaning "beautiful water." Here's an Iroquoian linguistic piece of trivia for anybody out there interested in such things: "*io*" on the end of any word, a suffix if you will, means something is beautiful (should you ever want to flirt with an Iroquoian woman, that's a handy scrap of information to know.) The city I live in, Toronto is another Iroquoian word meaning "gathering or meeting place." Manitoba, Saskatchewan and Nunavut are all Indigenous names. You get the point.

Most Aboriginal people now have English names. Drew Hayden

Taylor is not a proud Aboriginal name my great great great grandfathers would have understood or appreciated. The name does not come from the voice of the land. No doubt, it came from some English trader or Minister. Such is the price of colonization; to wear the clothes of the conquerors, and sing their songs.

Canada is famous for having two official languages, French and English. This is something which has always irked me. I don't remember being allowed to vote on that decision. I must have been in the bathroom or something. These two languages have been on this continent we call Turtle Island for approximately five hundred years, give or take a decade or two. The life span of a good sized tree. Five hundred years! That's three thousand five hundred in dog, or rather *nemush*, years.

Remember, there were over fifty separate Native languages and dialects in Canada alone when wayward lost travellers, starving and frightened, landed on our shores thinking they had reached Asia. Somehow that history has evolved into an often volatile language issue which Canadians frequently face. It is my personal opinion that Canada, a once simple group of huts, has many more than two official languages, with English and French merely the most recent trendy languages to wander the Canadian landscape. I may not be allowed back into Canada for saying that but what the hell, it's warmer here. It is said that when a tribal Elder dies, a library dies with them. When an Indigenous language dies, a philosophy dies. A way of thinking, a manner of human expression, an integral part of a Nation dies. As a person who does not speak my mother's language, the first in the long chain not to, I am part of that death. I have to live with that. Thank you for listening to my words... my English words.

There is no word for good-bye in the Ojibway language... only *Co-obmen* –I'll be seeing you.

WHAT'S IN A NAME?

North America is populated with people from the Four Directions of the Earth. As a result, it is rife with hybrid cultures –French Canadians, Mexican Americans and a host of other people who claim two different cultures as their heritage. Ahh. The mosaic of the Western Hemisphere. The First Nations people of this land are no different. They are also seen kayaking through that large genetic pool. Whether stationary, or nomadic in nature a sea-going people or Arctic settlers, the nature of interaction is bound to have unique cultural and biological consequences on Canada's Native People. I know of what I speak for I am half Ojibway and half Caucasian. Which makes me an "Occasion" or, as I frequently have been known to think of myself, a Special Occasion.

That said, imagine there are well over forty First Nations in Canada alone. Add to that the multitudes of oppressed masses and those from other parts of the globe who yearned to be free, and you get quite the melting pot. I know that is the popular American slogan, but we Native people don't recognize the border so I feel I can safely appropriate that terminology. Cruising the streets of Canada are people whose unorthodox lineage requires a new vocabulary to describe. For instance, an ex-girlfriend of mine was of Irish and Mohawk ancestry. That made her an "Ir-oqu" (Iroc). A good friend of mine in Calgary is a combination of Scottish, Chinese, Choctaw, and Norwegian, which, when combined makes him a "MacChinchoson". He says he never knows what to eat for dinner.

This is just the tip of the bi-cultural iceberg. Those of Jewish and Mohawk ancestry are "Shmohawk;" although in our communities, a "Shmohawk" may refer to anyone of Jewish and any Native background. It is the same with Italian and any Native blood; they're simply known as "Awapahos". Other mixed bloods to keep in mind are the Ojibway and the Irish, which can give you "Ojiberish." Put together a Haida and an Ojibway, and you get a "Haidaway." The offspring of a Cree and a Naskapi would be kind of "Cree-pi." A Blood and Micmac combination is rare, but if you look hard enough you might find a "Blac." An equally rare rainbow child born of a Blood and an Innu would simply be known as a "Blu." Any offspring born of Onondagan and a Peigan would be "Onagan" (on again), unless of course they're off again. However, put an Okanagan and an Odawa together and, geography aside, you just might get an "Okanawa." Forget the Métis; a French and Cree union would produce someone "Free." However, a French and Ojibway bi-product would be considered a "Freeway."

I'm sure somewhere is a family consisting of a Latin and a Dene and all their little "Lattes." At some pow wow I remember hearing about the marriage between a Deleware and a Tlingit which resulted in an adorable little "Delegit." I suppose a Cree/Mohawk union might offer a "Crock." Cross a Huron and a German and, believe it or not, you get a "Human." A French and Huron couple might produce some "Free-on." Combine Swedish chromosomes with Salish and it won't be long before you get a "Swish." On the same thought, the offspring of a Salish woman and an Ojibway man might make a "Salaway". A union of Irish and Micmac would get you a "Mcmicmac;" but I'm sure you already knew that one.

Noted writer Tom King, whose background is Cherokee and Greek, is proud to be known as a "Cherogreek." If you combine the backgrounds of the Potawatami and the Chipewayan you might find yourself with a "Potato Chip"

On a more complex note, if you combine the ancestry of a Chickasaw, Potawatami and a Piute, you'd get a tasty "Chicken Pot Pie."

You may think this exercise is strange but I remember some friends taking me to a restaurant while I was in New York City. They told me it was the best Cuban-Chinese restaurant in the city. That proved to me anything is possible.

WHERE DO I SIGN UP?

It has been said (and proven) that revolutionary principles and great ideas often come from places of higher education, like universities or colleges. Well, according to a very good friend of mine located in wonderful downtown Edmonton, the University of Alberta has done such a thing. Students there noticed that Native society, ever in a state of ebb and flow, was in need of a new social organization on campus; one that administers to the needs and wants of its wounded student body. Specifically, Native men in pain. The name of this new self help group is called S.A.W. which stands for Survivors of Aboriginal Women. Definitely a long needed support group with thousands of potential members.

According to my friend (who's capable of breaking quite a few hearts in her own right), this organization is set up to help men deal with the repercussions and recovery that resulted from dating Aboriginal women. The pain, the agony, the scolding, the tears - sort of a combination therapy group/frat house thing, I assume. Evidently, as a result of prior painful relationships, these men don't have hearts anymore, just scar tissue. My first reaction upon hearing of this organization was, "Where do I sign up?" I want to start a Toronto chapter. I feel their pain. If you can believe it, my ex-girlfriend once chewed me (*the bastard*) out for almost fifteen minutes because I returned a hamburger to the counter at Wendy's incorrectly.

Before you immediately dismiss the idea of such an organization as silly as a home for unwed Native fathers, try to picture, these delicate, wounded men sitting in a circle, hands on each other's shoulders, eyes gazing at each other sympathetically.

"Hi. My name is Ted, and I've dated a Cree.

"Hi Ted."

The next logical step would be to develop some sort of a twelve step program to be drafted into the charter. Indians like twelve step programs.

It should probably go something like this:

Step # 1:
Admit to yourself that Native women are beautiful and you are not at fault for falling in love with them.

Step # 2:
Admit that for every door that is slammed in your face,
another one will open... usually a divorce lawyer's.

Step # 3:
Love hurts. Some love more than others.

Step # 4:
It is not her fault that she broke your heart or your fishing
rod, or your pool cue. You will to live.

Step # 5:
Always remember... your mother is an Aboriginal woman
too.

Step # 6:
Without women in your life, the world would be a very
boring and gay place.

...and so on, seven through twelve, various other assorted
pearls of wisdom to ease the pain.

I applaud the University of Alberta for their fortitude in founding
such a gathering of kindred spirits. It probably won't get them many
dates, but that's not the point. We're talking about larger issues to be
wrestled with. There may be a little more "self-snagging" on the Pow
wow trail this summer but it's all for a good cause.

Wanting to know what women thought of S.A.W; I mentioned the
organization to a female acquaintance of mine. A glazed look fell over
her as she went through a quick assessment of past partners. Her
comment: "Geez, I bet I got a couple of ex's in there. Come to think
of it, they all drink Molsons Ex too." Another friend had a slightly
worried look. "They don't actually name names... do they? I gotta
make some phone calls." She then disappeared with her hand full of
quarters.

An organization such as this poses some interesting questions. Is
it strictly a men's organization with males bonding over female
troubles? Is the organization about dealing with female fraternization

recovery? This asks an even more interesting question... can lesbians join? I'm sure they have their share of women problems. How about people who have issues with their mothers? Transsexuals? The 21st Century can be so complicated.

Now I know what you're thinking. This came up frequently in my research. If there's a S.A.W, there has got to be a S.A.M., Survivors of Aboriginal Men. In fact, many would argue there's a more pressing need for a S.A.M. But it has also been argued that there is already a place where women congregate to discuss and complain about the current and past men in their lives. It's called Bingo.

RECREATIONAL CULTURAL APPROPRIATION

F. Scott Fitzgerald once wrote "The rich are different from you and me", to which everybody usually responds, "Yeah, they got more money." On a similar theme, it's been my Ojibway-tainted observation over the years that "Middle Class White people are different from you and I"... yeah, they're insane.

Much has been written over the years about the differences between Native people and non-Native people, and how differently they view life. I think there's no better example of this admittedly broad opinion than in the peculiar world of outdoor recreational water sports and the death wish that surrounds it. As a member of Canada's Indigenous population, I've always cast a suspicious glance at all these water-logged enthusiasts for several reasons. The principal one being the now familiar concept of cultural appropriation –this time of our methods of water transportation. On any given weekend, the Canadian rivers are jam packed with plastic/fibreglass kayaks and canoes, practically none of them filled with authentic Inuit or Native people, all looking to taunt death using an Aboriginal calling card.

Historically, kayaks and canoes were the life blood of most Native and Inuit communities. They were vital means of transportation and survival, not toys to amuse bored weekend beige warriors. To add insult to injury and further illustrate my point, there's a brand of gloves used by kayakers to protect their hands from developing callouses. There are called Nootkas. To the best of my knowledge, the real Nootka , a West Coast First Nation, neither kayaked nor wore gloves. Perhaps my argument can best be articulated with an example of the different ways of these two cultural groups react to a single visual stimulus. First, in a river, you put some Native people in a canoe, right beside some White people in a canoe. Directly in front of them should be a long stretch of roaring rapids. With large pointy rocks and lots and lots of turbulent white water. Now watch the different reactions.

Granted, I'm being a bit general but I think I can safely say the vast majority of Native people, based on thousands of years of traveling the rivers of this great country of ours, would probably go home and order a pizza. Or possibly put the canoe in their Ford pickup and drive down stream to a more suitable and safe location. And pick up pizza on the way. Usually, the only white water Native people prefer is in their showers. Hurtling towards potential death and certain injury tends to go against many traditional Native beliefs. Contrary to popular belief, the word portage is not a French word, its Native for "Are you crazy?! I'm not going through that! Do you know how much I paid for this canoe?"

Now you put some sunburned Caucasian canoeists in the same position, their natural inclination is to aim directly for the rapids paddling as *fast* as they can *towards* the white water. I heard a rumour once that Columbus was aiming his three ships directly at a raging hurricane when he discovered the Bahamas. I believe I have made my point. Yet even with this bizarre lemming-like behavior, there are still more White people out there than Native people.

I make these observations based on personal experience. Recently, for purely anthropological reasons, I have risked my life to explore this unique sub-culture known as white water canoeing and sea kayaking. There is also a sport known as white water kayaking but I have yet to put that particular bullet in my gun. So for three days I found myself in the middle of Georgian Bay during a storm testing my abilities at sea kayaking. I, along with a former Olympic rower, a Québécois lawyer who consulted on the Russian Constitution, one of Canada's leading Diabetes specialists, and a 6 foot 7 inch tall ex-Mormon who could perform exorcisms, bonded over four foot swells and lightening. All in all, I think a pretty normal crosscut of average Canadians. The higher the waves, the more exciting they found it.

Still, I often find these outings to be oddly very patriotic in their own unique way. I cannot tell you the number of times I've seen many of these people wringing out their drenched shirts, showing an unusual array of tan lines, usually a combination of sunburnt red skin, and fish-belly white stomachs. For some reason, it always reminds me of the red and white motif on the Canadian flag. Maybe, back in the 1960s, that's where the Federal government got their original inspiration for our national emblem.

But this is only one of several sports originated by various Indigenous populations that have been corrupted and marketed as something fun to do when not sitting at a desk in some high rise office building. The Scandinavian Sami, otherwise known as Laplander were very instrumental in the development of skiing, though I doubt climbing to the top of a mountain and hurling themselves off it to make it to the bottom as fast as gravity and snow would allow, was not a culturally ingrained activity. The same could be said for Bungee jumping. Originally a coming of age ritual in the south Pacific, young boys would build platforms, tie a vine to their leg and leap off to show their bravery and passage into adulthood. I doubt the same motivation still pervades in the sport, if it can be called a sport.

I have brought this issue of recreational cultural appropriation up many times with my friend who usually organizes these outdoor adventures. The irony is, she works at a hospital. And she chews me out for not wearing a helmet while biking. She says there is no appropriation. If anything, her enthusiasm for these sports is a sign of respect and gratefulness.

That is why I think these people should pay a royalty of sorts every time they try to kill themselves using one of our cultural legacies. I'm not sure if a patent or copyright was ever issued on kayaks or canoes, it was probably conveniently left out of some treaty somewhere, but somebody should definitely investigate that possibility. Or better yet, I think that every time some non-Native person white water canoes down the Madawaska River, or goes kayaking off of Tobermory, they should first take an Aboriginal person to lunch. That is a better way of showing respect and gratefulness. And it's less paperwork.

THE POLITICS OF PARTYING

There are mysterious dealings afoot in the city of Toronto and in the country of Canada. I am puzzled over them. Aboriginal Solidarity Day came and went on June 21st with a fair amount of cultural celebrating and identity embracing across the country. This annual event provides the opportunity for thousands of Native people from all Nations to stand tall and shout to the world, "We are Native, Aboriginal, First Nations, Indigenous, and proud!" For the first time in months Aboriginal people made the news without any reference to the New Governance Act or their homes being endangered by forest fires. It was truly a good day to be Indian. And bonus, we got a day off work!

Hot on its heels came Gay Pride Week, an equally celebratory occasion but fraught with fabulous parades, outrageous makeup, and far too many questionable fashion decisions. This particular week is a tradition in Toronto and other major cities in Canada Two-Spirited people (as they are known in the Native community) get the chance to proudly state "We are Gay, Lesbians, Fags, Homosexuals, Dykes, and proud!" It was a good week to be Gay.

Two groups of proud people taking time out of their busy schedule to have a little fun, while at the same time do some public relations. My question, as a representative of the Indigenous community, is, why do they get a week and we Native people only get a day? Who do I have to complain to about getting this grievously disproportionate holiday allocation re-examined? Granted, we may lack a dazzling ability to properly colour-scheme a room, but the wearing of elaborate feathers and leather started with this country's original inhabitants long before the "Queer As Folk" television series. Yet, we only get one measly day... unless you happen to be a Gay Aboriginal then you get eight days in total to celebrate... but that's a different story.

After years of pondering, I have a theory that might better illuminate the issue. My theory is that someone somewhere is using a double axis graph or a calculating table specifically set up to assess the number of days to celebrate, by comparing the amount of cultural and social oppression each group has faced. Sort of a liberal social adjustment scale. There is no doubt in my mind that there is an obscure government ministry called the Department of Festivities for the

Socially and Historically Inconvenienced. But still, that doesn't answer my question of why only one day for Natives and seven for gays. I'm no accountant but I've seen enough treaties misinterpreted to know those numbers are wrong. I have nothing against Gay Pride Day; some of my best friends are gay and most of them are proud. It's more of a case of "Why does Billy get seven tank tops, while Jimmy Harvest Moon gets only one pair of rubber boots?" To me it's a matter of what is fair.

Several years back I remember a parade held on Aboriginal Solidarity Day in Toronto which was organized by actor/activist Gary Farmer. The festival was called Buffalo Jump, named after one of our unique ways of hunting Buffalo. The Plains people used to stampede a buffalo herd toward a hidden cliff where they fell to their death. I don't know if this was exactly the best metaphor for holding a parade.

Then there's the African-Canadian community who get a whole month of recognition. Granted, it is held the month of February, one of the coldest of the year, but it is substantially more than a mere one day. Twenty-eight days, not including leap year is better than one lone day or seven pride-filled days. We get twenty-four hours to celebrate thousands upon thousands of years of history, culture, and land claims. I think a parliamentary committee should be set up to investigate this oversight.

Now I'm sure political heavyweights like the Canadian Alliance along with other right wing organizations (the ones you won't see marching in the Gay Pride Parade) probably think there's already too much cultural observance on the yearly calender as it is. They might be thinking, 'Where is the celebration of the people that make this country great? Where is the mighty WASP parade instead of ones for those degenerates and immigrants?' (Some people believe Native people fit into either category). Maybe they will take solace in a bit of homespun wisdom I received as a child on my Reserve. I remember asking my mother why there was a Father's Day and a Mother's Day but no Children's Day. And I was told that "Every day is Children's Day." If this is true and we acknowledge the existence of Aboriginal Solidarity Day, Gay Pride Week and Black Awareness Month, I suppose the remaining days in the calender are Caucasian Days... excluding St. Patrick's Day and Jean Baptiste Day – two more one day Ethnic wonders. I'm not quite sure where the Irish and French-

Canadians sit in the oppression spectrum.

I'm sure many people would argue that gays and lesbians flaunt their sexuality all the time, but what about those poor, downtrodden heterosexuals who want their moment in the sun. You don't see signs advertising "Come celebrate Straight Week," although Spring Break comes close. It might be rationalized that everyday is Heterosexual Day. Now that Gay Pride Week has come and gone, have a happy Heterosexual/Caucasian Day. Let me know where the golf tournament and Barbecue is taking place. I'll bring the Indians.

WHAT MAKES AN ABORIGINAL AN ABORIGINAL?

Not that long ago, I read an article written by an incensed mixed blood Maori woman who had been asked how much Maori blood she had. "I have just as much blood as any other Maori woman" she wrote defiantly. Unfortunately, not everyone understands such a simple concept. In the modern age, the definition of what is Native and what isn't is continually being wrestled with.

Case in point, Jewish/American film maker Marc Halberstadt has developed an interesting documentary project about his family. Like thousands of others, they were driven out of Germany prior to the Second World War. The Halberstadts are currently involved in getting compensation for their house and a successful business lost in the tragedy. The irony is that he ended up in a country where the Indigenous people are attempting the same thing; compensation for lost land our story inspired him. In his documentary, Halberstadt wants to bring together a group of five Native comedians and send them to Germany with the purpose of knocking on the doors of both the home and the business his family once owned. Their purpose is to say to the startled occupants, "Hi. Sorry to bother you, but evidently you owe some people in America compensation money. Indirectly, the people in America owe us compensation money, so we thought we'd elimi-nate the middle men and you can pay us directly." Related to the project is an anticipated audience with the Pope and an additional trip to Israel to deal with similar issues. For the past few months, he's been feverishly auditioning and interviewing funny Indian people across North America, to come up with a potentially dangerous mix of humour, knowledge of guerrilla theatre, and lots of chutspah to pull this off properly. This is where the story takes a unique turn.

While scouring Canada, he became engaged in discussions with myself and a young actor/improv artist named Ryan McMahon. Halberstadt was shocked at how fair both Ryan and I were. He said that, if we were included in the documentary, nobody would know we were Native. Was there even a point in putting us in the documentary? He thought it would be more shocking for the Germans to open their door and find a long haired, dark-skinned Native looking person dripping in melatonin and leather. Some would argue Ryan and I look more German than Native, but after almost four decades of hearing

25

similar comments, I've sort of gotten used to it. Ryan is in the unique position of trying to validate existence as a mixed blood person to this American/German film maker. It made him uncomfortable. I felt this issue added a different kind of irony to the documentary concept, something akin to "We have been colonized right down to a genetic level, so you don't just owe us land claim compensation, you also owe child support."

The issue became a rather focal one, with many calls made back and forth on how it should be handled. I found it odd that racial politics was getting in the way of a racially political documentary. Halberstadt eventually decided that if he had three Native looking people in the cast (the Dances with Wolves kind), he could probably get away with two homogeneous ones, (the Val Kilmer kind).

This sense of toleration, of making allowances for mixed bloods, has been an issue of severe annoyance. This past summer, there appeared a light at the end of this myopic tunnel. This light came from Maniwaki, Quebec, where I was attending an event called the "Gathering of All Nations" to shoot a documentary on William Commanda, the Algonquin Elder who hosts the gathering. On Saturday morning, he delivered an interesting speech, where he made reference to the fifth race, or colour of man. In most First Nation cultures, we are taught the world has four races Red, Yellow, Black and White. The Medicine Wheel is divided into coloured quarters to represent those four important citizens of the Earth. Commanda said a fifth race needs to be included. Mixed bloods, on what he referred to as the Blue Race deserve a place in the Medicine Wheel.

I had never heard that concept before and it made an impression on me. I have always told people that in this complicated world my origins were quite simple. And used a wine metaphor to explain. There is red and white wine but me and my compatriots are a mixture –a rose or blush wine. I was wrong, we are blue. This is great for me since it matches my eyes. I'm not sure if I'd want to drink that colour of a wine but you get my point.

Doing the documentary in Germany sounds like it will be a fun trip and could be something ground-breaking, but I haven't decided if I want to go. I think Ryan isn't sure yet either. It is an intriguing concept... five Indians let loose in Germany with an expense account... might be nothing left in compensation.

INDIANS IN SPACE!

It wasn't that long ago when the Aboriginal media was raving about the launch of the first person of Native ancestry to be launched into space aboard the Space Shuttle Endeavour. His name is Commander John Herrington, a member of Oklahoma's Chickasaw tribe. I believe he took an eagle feather with him on his historic flight. He boldly went where no Aboriginal had gone before. He took one small step for man, one giant step for First Nations. He must have thought "today is a good day to fly." His heart (and the rest of him) really did soar like an eagle. Aye Captain, the Injins canna take it!... and so on and so on. This event caused me to ponder the concept of Native people and outer space. Now there's two things you rarely see in the same sentence. First Nation people are seldom thought of when it comes to space technology or science fiction. Come to think of it, neither are country music and bannock, hmmm... I wonder if there's a connection.

There is, Chakotey from the Star Trek Voyager series; but, most would agree he's more of a Latino with a bad tattoo. They've never really defined what nation he comes from, although there are tantalizing hints that he's Central American with possible Aztec or Mayan roots. I love the palm pilot thingee he has that speeds up vision quests. It's quite a remarkable device. Place it in your hand, turn it on, and in a few minutes you're communing with your spirit guide or ancestors. In terms of vision/dream quests, it's quite the little time saver. I want one. Fasting for days can really eat away at your space exploration time. It's a pity there's no such gadget for land claim settlements.

Other than Commander Herrington, the skies and stars are a little lean on Native influences. Perhaps it's because Native people are often thought of as being more historical in reference. When the public thinks of us, it's often in terms of the vanishing Indian. Even today they imagine images of yesteryear: living in teepees, riding horses, chasing buffalo –all that nostalgic stuff. When we think of ourselves, it is also often in terms of the past and of all the things we've lost in the last five hundred years: land, language, customs, resources. In terms of our future, we always seem to be looking back to the past to recover what we lost.

What does the future hold for the Aboriginal population of North America? Who can say? On a philosophical level, the possibilities of

27

space travel do present some interesting questions for those traditional Indians who might want to consider a life above and beyond Turtle Island. For instance, one of the things that have made us strong and allowed us to survive all those years of oppression is our connection to the land. It's one of our strongest beliefs. Now, the question of the moment is, is it just this land or will any land do? Does Mars count as Mother Earth? Mother Mars perhaps. Will we take that connection to Turtle Island with us to other parts of this universe? How will that change our beliefs?

What about this whole concept of colonization? Imagine our Native astronauts landing on some far-off land, and saying, "We claim this land in the name of...Turtle Island...?!?" Will our ancestors be spinning in their graves if we end up suckling on the colonial teat too? Heaven forbid if there's an indigenous species living on that planet. That would scald the bottom of the corn soup pot for sure. Is there a traditional teaching or an Assembly of First Nations policy to address this potential situation?

For instance, what would happen if we managed to design, construct and launch our own space ship or space station. Like the Space Shuttle Buffy St. Marie or Space Station Kahliga. The problems would begin almost immediately. First of all, tradition dictates we would have a sweetgrass ceremony (or sage or tobacco) to bless the place in the closed environment of space with all sorts of fire suppression gadgetry about. Smoke is a definite no-no in the closed quarters of interstellar existence. Plus, the concentrated levels of oxygen might make things a little more dangerous.

More puzzling, how can you honour the Four Directions when there are no directions? Do you choose four directions arbitrarily? Perhaps a larger constant, like using the plane of the solar system, or even the galaxy itself? Or maybe we could use some complicated computerized method of relating Earth-based directions to your current position on board what ever it is you're on board of. I don't remember Chakotey having these problems.

It's all so complicated. Maybe that's why we never bothered to think about it. Horses and buffalo are easier to deal with.

Holidaze and Birthdaze
(the Operative Word Being Daze)

OLDER AND A LITTLE WISER

I am now 40 years old –14,600 days or 350,400 hours and counting. This Earth on which I sit writing has traveled completely around the sun (an enormous distance when you think of it) forty times and now on it's way to forty-one times to the other side of the sun and back. That is an unfathomable distance in jogging terms. And in that time, disco, punk and grunge have come and gone; bell bottoms, leisure suits, and pastel t-shirts are now memories of the past; and *The Beachcombers, Mr. Dressup* and *The Tommy Hunter Show* burned brightly as pinnacles of Canadian artistic expression(and then been cancelled).

As I enter my fifth decade, thoughts of mortality and life's true meaning have recently bounced around in my head pondering and questioning why we do things and why things happen to us and generally thinking, what the hell do I do now... frequently engages my consciousness. Perhaps I should preface this by mentioning that I don't have a hang-up about getting old, but, as any therapist or counsellor may tell you, a little soul searching is good for what ails you. And turning forty is as good a reason as any to plumb your personal depths.

Out of curiosity, I once checked the archives at a university library to see what happened on the day of my birth way back in the summer of 1962. The front page of the Toronto Star mentions a huge Shriners convention and a parade. Wonderful! I was born during the year of the Shriner. Maybe that's why I drink so much.

Granted, many people tell me that at the age of forty (280 in dog years), I'm still a baby, a pup, why practically a kid. The problem here is that most of the people saying this are older than me. I'm not sure if they're trying to reassure me or themselves. Pondering this all came to a head several weeks ago when I visited the place I grew up and took a nostalgic walk through this little community nestled in the heart of central Ontario. I found myself walking past my grandparents' old house next to it was the apple tree I, as a child, practically lived and which had the best apples in the village. I looked at it like I would an old friend, a dying old friend, since half of the branches were dead and the rest didn't look like they would had be too long in this world.

On the other side of the house grew a stand of cedar trees.

Because of the way cedar seeds are clumped together, it's not uncommon for a number of trees to grow together. This stand of trees always reminded me of an open hand lying on the ground with five or six tree-fingers growing skyward and an open palm at the center. I spent long hours playing in this natural fort. They were now dead too. I'd always been told that trees live for hundreds of years. "My God," I thought, "I'm outliving trees." Still, these past four decades have taught me a few things, most of which I was happy to learn.

Case in point, the ominous and foreboding world of dating. Having recently been summarily and suddenly dismissed from my former fiance's life, I once again have been forced out into the breeding pool of society, this time a little older and a little more wary. Time to blow the dust off of my old lines. I may have to update my standard "Guns and Roses. What a band huh?" After almost twenty-five years of dating experience, I think I've finally got a handle on this whole *finding-a-partner* game we all play with varying amounts of success.

It has been my experience that in our youth, we are often captivated by a stunningly beautiful face or figure. At times our souls are commandeered by a devilish sense of humour or we become intrigued by an individual's insight and intelligence. Back in those early days, those were enough. And then down the road, because we were so blinded by a particularly overwhelming feature, the brightness begins to fade and we see other things (or a lack of things) in those we've pledged to love. It's very rare we will find several of those intrinsic attributes rolled up into one very special person, that rare person you want to spend the rest of your life with.

Oddly enough, I equate this analysis of dating with track and field. For example, you have your long distance runners, your shot putters, your hop-skip-and-jumpers, all fantastic in their own world of expertise, but try to get a long distance runner to throw a javelin and you'll be disappointed. Pretty soon, the novelty wears off and you're stuck watching marathons for the rest of your life.

I, on the other hand, have decided in my declining years that when next I start dating, I want somebody who can and will win the decathlon. The principle behind the decathlon being somebody that may not be the best discuss thrower or sprinter, but they are more than good enough at each different sport to score enough points to be

31

judged best overall athlete. In reality, it's much harder to be a decent decathloner than to excel at any one sport. It takes determination, tremendous talent and the ability to multi-focus. Why should I settle for less in the dating world?

I'd also be content with a decent Ironman (or rather, Ironwoman) competitor too –runner, biker, and swimmer –because a successful relationship is definitely a marathon. It also involves keeping your balance and making sure the mechanisms of the relationship is well oiled. And finally, keeping your head above water to see where you're going because if you keep your head down and underwater, you could get lost.

It took me forty years to learn this. Next on my list is learning to work the VCR.

AN ABORIGINAL CHRISTMAS PERSPECTIVE

Ask any Native person what they want for Christmas and they might tell you their land back, an end to economic and social racism, or possibly better cable selection. And what do I want this holiday season? I want this festive season to bring me a better understanding of the love/hate relationship Native people have with Christianity and its celebratory offshoots. Oh, and a new computer.

This seasonal quest for knowledge came to me just last week when I made a pilgrimage to the General Synod Archives for the Anglican Church of Canada located on Jarvis Street in Toronto. Ironically, I was scheduled to pick up photographs of Aboriginal Residential schools and their students/conscripts for a documentary for the National Film Board. Oddly enough, the documentary is on Native erotica. Immediately upon entering into the lobby, I felt uncomfortable and ill at ease; a feeling I've encountered before while touring other religious edifices. It is a feeling that someone is watching you, knows what you've been up to and knows that Native people believe in living in harmony with Nature, not having dominion over it as indicated in the Bible. The sensation stayed with me until I left the building and had made my way down the street. Makes one wonder if Christian churches and organizations can carry bad Karma.

Consciously, part of me began wondering if this was a uniquely Native thing –to be aware of the ghosts of generations of Aboriginal people who had the word of God beaten into them, were kidnapped from their families and abused, in order to be shown the way to Heaven. The missionary zeal of "Worship our God (or we'll beat you until you do)" tends to leave a bad aftertaste. The Golden Rule, "Do unto others as you would have them do unto you" must have been edited out of the North American edition of the operator's guide to civilizing heathens.

However, after some serious pondering (in a coffee shop, of course), I came to realize that my questionable appreciation of such theological organizations is not unique to just the Aboriginal people of this continent. Many different cultures over the world had religious orthodoxy forced upon them by conquering nations. That was part of the inspiration for Columbus' voyages and the Islamic expansion during the 7th Century. Remember, history and hymns are written by the winners.

After Cortez's destruction of the Aztec Empire, the Spanish government, along with the Pope's blessing, decided to instigate what was called the Requiermento. Feeling a little guilty over the rampant destruction of Central American civilizations, Church and State decided to give the people a chance, a voice, in their own destruction. As conquering Conquistadores marched into the Aboriginal villages, there was someone at the head of the column who read aloud from the Requiermento, a proclamation telling all citizens of the village they had a choice of voluntarily becoming vassals of the Pope and Spanish King or to be utterly destroyed. A minor point is that the document was read in Spanish. Needless to say, the ability to choose did little to stop their destruction. Felis Navidad.

Soon, the introduction of Christmas to the Americas with its message of peace and love, came between waves of epidemics and forcible relocations. This unique co-existence has remained until today, resulting in groups of Native people both suspicious and loyal to the Church. A confusing, though understandably, schizophrenic existence.

I've been lucky enough to travel to over 120 Native communities across Canada and the U.S. The most unusual thing I have seen in many poor and economically disadvantaged communities, are two financially disproportionate displays of wealth –satellite dishes and massive Christmas lights and holiday adornment on houses that appear barely strong enough to hold them up.

Christmas, commonly viewed by most historians as a pagan rite dressed up in a priest's collar, is a hard tradition to turn down regardless of the sexual abuse its progenitors condoned in the aforementioned schools. Native people have a soft spot for stories about babies being born, and it really wasn't *HIS* fault what happened two thousand years later.

Most of my family loves Christmas, as does practically every Native community in Canada. Even the ones hurt and damaged by the effects of Residential schools. Christmas carols really are that addictive. Even the more traditional communities that embrace First Nations beliefs still get a week off from work during the Yuletide season. Eggnog knows no spiritual boundaries. Personally, I still like

Christmas, although I hold no particular allegiance to Jesus Christ or Santa Claus, two popular White men with far too much say in the Native community. I hum the carols when I hear them on the radio. I spend way too much money on gifts. My blood sugar level drifts dangerously close to the endemic diabetes that is constantly knocking on the Aboriginal door. The bottom line is that Christmas is fun. Any man who's willing to die for your sins (and there are plenty of them on both sides of the ecclesiastical line) is worth roasting a turkey for.

Just think; if Jesus were around today and was Native, he'd probably be in therapy from Residential school trauma. Happy Birthday, Buddy.

THE WRITTEN WORD CAN BE HEAVY LUGGAGE

Once again I'm in the position of having to move house and body. Like many people who occasionally become nomadic, I find myself looking with foreboding at the shelves upon shelves upon shelves of books which line my walls. I have never counted them, but I'm sure they number into the high hundreds, maybe even thousands. Eventually, they will have to be boxed, carried and unloaded somewhere in the city, probably with several large groans and yet another impotent promise to myself that nothing short of a nuclear war will ever make me move again.

At various stages in my life I have been told (or more accurately been heartily suggested) by friends who have helped me move that perhaps I should consider being a little less protective of my books, or be a little less packrattish. As one poor friend asked under the weight of my Stephen King collection, "What good are they once you've read them?"

I could probably make a small fortune if I were to descend upon some luckless (or very lucky, depending on your point of view) second-hand book store with my volumes of stories, but that could also potentially devastate our already battered stock market; stocks in used book stores would plummet with the glut of books suddenly dumped into the market. I have too much respect for our Canadian economy to let that happen. Besides, I have a unique relationship with all my books and keep them close for a number of reasons. They are memories of a conquered world, each book representing a trophy of accomplishments. I keep them on their shelves in the vain belief that, someday I will find the time to read them once again when all other books in the universe have been destroyed. They are my friends.

Then again, maybe my human friends are right in that I'm being a little too melodramatic when it comes to a few ounces of paper and ink. My grandparents thought that too. During my teenage years, they said quite seriously to my mother, "You shouldn't let him read so much. It's not normal." When you're the only child of a single mother growing up on an Ojibway Reserve in the 1970s, your options for entertainment are somewhat limited. I was reading John Wyndham and H.G. Wells between episodes of *Welcome Back Kotter*.

Today, my library is a little more varied. Soon, I'll be crating books ranging from nostalgically cherished trashy sci-fi to a variety of almanacs and reference books to an amazing collection of Native literature to many of the classics, including a signed copy of Arthur Miller's *Death Of A Salesman*.

Is it worth it? Purchasing the books themselves is fairly expensive. So are the bookshelves used to store them. Replacing the ones friends borrow, honestly promising they'll return them, can also cost a few bucks. And when I move, the men, time and truck used to cart them from place to place undoubtedly adds up to an uncomfortable fee. All this for books, some which I have literally (no pun intended) not opened in twenty years. Of course it's worth it.

I remember visiting a friend for dinner years ago. Something in their house nagged at my subconscious. It took a while but I finally realized there were no books visible anywhere in the house, no bookshelves in the living room, no coffee-table books or even magazines on the coffee table, not even a cookbook in the kitchen. The only paper was in the bathroom –toilet paper. Their house was devoid of any kind of literature. It seemed barren.

Call me biased, but for me, it is books that help to make a home. How many of us, upon entering a house, quickly scan the bookshelves to get a speedy grasp of where these people's minds are and where they let their imagination take them? I know I do.

At least one thing will give me some solace when I start packing my books; all that reading and all those books gave me the opportunity impetus to become a writer. Somewhere out there are eleven books I have been lucky enough to have published. Further out there are masses of other people packing to move their homes and bodies. Hopefully, they are grunting and groaning over a box of these books.

A WHITE CHRISTMAS

The mobs in the malls, the cacophony of carols, and the peculiar preoccupation with evergreen trees warns me that yet again, the season known as Christmas has arrived once more –here to baffle all of us poor Aboriginals with a confusing array of mixed messages. The Yuletide season could use an edition of "Christmas for Dummies."

Prior to contact, in the time known as B.C. (i.e. Before Christmas), winter was not exactly seen as a time of happiness and plenty for most First Nations in Canada. It was a time of survival, of difficult trials. Gifts of snowballs and ice, all that was usually found in moccasins hung to dry. Drafty wigwams, longhouses and teepees typically meant Jack Frost nipped at more than just your nose. Dashing through the snow meant you were chasing dinner. Eight tiny reindeer could just about feed the whole village.

Civilization then came to this continent and brought a remarkably complicated concept known as Christmas. As years went by, it gradually evolved into two different branches of Christmas... much like the two different kinds of Christianity that also evolved over the past two thousand years. I'm being extremely conservative in specifying only two branches of Christian belief, but if I named all the various Christian sects that once and currently exist with their big toe in or out of the Christmas pie, Christmas would be over and I'd be writing about the Easter Bunny.

In the world of Christianity, one form of Christmas deals with the actual Christ being born of a Virgin so the children of this world would have context for the songs "Away in A Manger" and "Silent Night, Holy Night".

Christ's birth as the Son of God is still celebrated in many Native communities, as well as all over the world. Yet, while the message is about universal peace, more wars have been fought in the name of God (with or without his Son) than any other reason. 'Tis the season to be jolly. Like I said before, Christmas can be very confusing for a Indigenous not so versed in the intricate logic of this festive season.

The second, more commercial aspect of Christmas involves other wonderful gifts brought to us by Western Civilization, specifically, the concepts of private property and the elaborate and unbending English legal system; both which teach that a man's home is his castle. And our land is now his moat. Now this has something to do with a rather portly Caucasian man with an affinity for showing his disdain for several long-cherished North American beliefs.

With the introduction of private property and the numerous laws to ensure its legality, this man makes a yearly habit of breaking and entering practically every house in the civilized world and getting away with complete impunity. He is obviously a rebel and a radical who has little consideration for the law. Not only that, but in this continent's capitalistic economic system, he maintains and promotes his socialist own beliefs by leaving presents for children regardless of their economic status. Because of this left-wing bias, he is often referred to as "the man in red."

The contradictory aspect of this rotund philanthropist is even more confusing than the man born in a manger. The rampant redistribution of wealth is based solely on his own culturally specific Caucasian perception of "Who has been naughty or nice," notably very subjective standards, on both personal and societal levels. A point proven by the often poorer quality and limited number of the presents distributed to Native, Afro-Canadian, and other ethnic groups who occupy the lower levels of the economic ladder. There is definite favoritism for those in a more blessed financial and racial environment. So what gives with this man and this holiday? Can't these promoters of Christmas get their stories straight?

Times have certainly changed. When I was young, we used to leave milk and cookies out for Santa Claus after going to Church. Today, most of my Aboriginal friends are lactose intolerant, or diabetic, or afraid of the Church for certain Residential reasons. Damn confusing holiday; this Christmas.

IT'S NOT JUST AN AGE, IT'S A STATE OF MIND

What does one normally do on their 41st birthday? Blow out candles, read birthday cards, too I suppose. Put up with half-hearted birthday greetings from various friends and acquaintances. And, let's not forget pondering one's own mortality. Turning forty was traumatic enough, but it was more akin to going for a swim in a chilly lake, cold, and shocking but manageable. Add one extra year and there are no more excuses. You just jump completely into the bone chilling river of your fifth decade of existence. You. Are. Completely. In. Your. Forties. Abandon all hope. This year seems unusually aggressive in its attempt to welcome me into that decade. The gods are letting me know I am entering a new phase of my life. Recently, I went to a play with a friend, and her eight-year-old daughter. On the way home, this little girl looked at me and innocently asked how old I was. I told her. She paused for a moment then responded, "Wow, my grandmother is only eight years older than you." That hurt. It still hurts.

Shortly after, a lovely woman asked me out on a date. She was twenty years-old. (For a moment I was flattered. "I still have it" I thought). Then a startling revelation occurred to me. I was in high school when she was born. I was chasing girls when she was chasing rubber balls. Not wanting to be rude, I accepted her invitation. I have many faults in life, but being an "ageist" is not one of them. So, we started seeing each other, and on one of our dates, we went to work out at the YMCA. You really don't know a person until you've seen them sweat. We got on adjoining treadmills and imputed our information into the gizmo (speed, weight, incline). I jokingly commented that running on the treadmill reminded me of the opening credits of The Six Million Dollar Man, where the treadmill he's running on shows sixty miles an hour. Not hearing a response, I looked over and saw complete confusion on her face. She had never seen the Six Million Dollar Man television show, had never heard of Steve Austin, Lee Majors or bionics. That also hurt. It still hurts. I hurt a lot.

Perhaps the most searing pain to hit me this year came from an academic source. I was at a Native literature conference at the University of Windsor, when a gentleman walked up to Daniel David Moses and I at a wine and cheese party. He introduced himself as a professor from the University. He said he was delighted to meet us as he had taught both of our dramatic works in his theatre history class. It was official –it was not a regular history class but a theatre history class course! That really hurt. It still does. Thank god there was wine.

But what can you do? Aging is a part of life. You cannot fear the inevitable, death, taxes and all that. Getting older becomes increasingly more inconvenient as evidence of the past follows you around. For instance, I've dated ladies from Wikwemikong, Tyendinaga, Moraviantown, Nova Scotia, B.C, and various other communities. There are 633 Reserves in Canada but the list is beginning to get a little thin. I'm running out of Reserves I can visit.

One thing that does allow me to get up in the mornings and face the day are the little victories I can claim against the inevitable march of time and age. Last month when I was home on the Reserve, a friend asked me at the last moment to attend a wedding. It was summer and I had only brought a t-shirt and shorts with me. Not discouraged, my friend, who is a little older than me, took it upon herself to find me suitable clothing for the wedding dance. When she asked what size pants I wore, I told her I had a thirty-two-inch waist. She burst out laughing. Evidently I was the only forty-one-year-old man on the Reserve who could claim such an accomplishment. Even one of my cousins, who is about thirteen years younger than me, and my height, could only muster a thirty-six inch waist... and on the eighth day, God created the Stairmaster.

A few days later, after visiting the gym, I rushed home and threw on an old t-shirt I had hanging around the house, and went to visit this same friend. Bad idea. The t-shirt I put on was from a television show I had worked on when I was starting out sixteen years ago, called Spirit Bay. She recognized the t-shirt and growled at me, "How dare you wear a sixteen-year-old t-shirt into this house, one that you can still fit!!" Since then, she has not returned any of my calls.

There's no point in whining. Instead, I shall lie back and try to find that inner glow, which the Elders we all know and love have. I am not an Elder, and I still haven't found that inner glow yet, but I refuse to play shuffleboard or comment on how they just don't write music like they used to. And, there are still plenty of reservations to visit in the States.

SAME SEX MARRIAGES
Everybody Looks Alike In The Dark

I live at Church and Wellesley in downtown Toronto. As a result, there are two things that become rather apparent when I ponder my location of habitation. First being it's very hard to get a date with a woman in this neighbourhood because the bars, shops and patios are woefully lean of the feminine sex. Second it is related directly to the first. Those same bars, shops and patios are overflowing with an awful lot of gay men who live, socialize and drink a heck of a lot of coffee at the local Second Cup; all within a few blocks of my apartment. I am a stranger in a strange land: a heterosexual in the Gay village. As Seinfeld says, "Not that there's anything wrong with it." It just makes me feel fatter and in definite need of a wardrobe upgrade.

I was at ground zero on June 10th, 2003 when the Ontario Court of Appeals passed a decision that broadened the definition of marriage to include same sex partners which allowed homosexuals and lesbian the opportunity to enjoy the dubious benefits of matrimony. And as the cart follows the horse, no doubt they have right to eventually divorce. The yin and yang of legalized sex.

British Columbia followed suit by passing a similar law on July 8th, 2003. Similar judicial decisions are expected in the near future from other provinces. Fallout was instantaneous and widespread. Religious leaders damned Prime Minister Jean Chretien's very soul for not stepping in to maintain the original "male/female" designation of a married couple. Editorials were written, protests and marches carried out, talk shows fighting the battle on the airwaves; all because the idea of two men or two women getting married gave some people the heebie jeebies. Eating liver gives me the heebie jeebies but you don't see me making a federal case out of it. Literally.

Call me cynical but these are people who need a serious reality check. Or, at the very least, to make up their minds about what they find so abhorrent. One of the major criticisms of same sex marriage cites a supposed rampant promiscuity present in the gay lifestyle. And that it would make a mockery of the marriage vows. Well, I assume any couple that wants to marry and share their life together would probably frown on either partner continuing a wild lifestyle. I assume the same love and fidelity embraced in a hetero marriage makes the decision to marry so appealing to all people, regardless of sexual persuasion. And heaven forbid, straight couples have absolutely no history of sexual abandon, and disrespecting that line about being faithful. None what so ever.

The only difference between alimony and palimony is the addition of the sixteenth letter of the alphabet. Adultery knows no sexual preference. Nagging is universal. Lets face it, this country has more important issues than where Steve and Bruce register for their china pattern. (Leaving the toilet seat up would not be grounds for divorce.)

Of course, none of this changes the fact that I still can't get a date in my neighbourhood.

43

COMING TO AMERICA

I have been to OZ. Actually walked the hallways. Not many people can say that. I am not referring to the prison on the television show or some place over the rainbow. It is the Mashantucket Pequot Reservation in Connecticut that I am referring to –home of not only the first but the largest recreational Aboriginal casino in North America. It is a large, imposing green structure rising majestically from the forest primeval as you drive into the community along the highway. And because of it's appearance and obvious potential to bestow dreams, local residents refer to the awe-inspiring building simply as Oz.

This particular visit occurred on my most recent trip south of the border and reinforced my humble opinion that America, even post September 11th, is truly a wacky and amusing place. Luckily, the last dozen years or so have offered me the opportunity to visit various sections of the United States fairly frequently. Each trip, like a stamp in a passport, leaves me with truly unique memories of our southern sister. And it is often the small things you remember that say so much.

Did you know that the state motto in New Hampshire is "Live Free Or Die?" It's on all their license plates. Live Free Or Die. That seems to be the only two choices currently available in that little pocket of New England. Kind of puts Ontario's "Yours To Discover" or Quebec's *"La Belle Province"* to shame, don't you think?

Tulsa, Oklahoma holds a special place in my heart. It has some of the best Art Deco architecture in the world, was the home town of one of America's leading porn stars, Stacy Valentine (or so I've heard), and for each of the three nights I was there for a theatre opening, there was a severe tornado warning. There's that Oz theme again. I sat in my room, looking out at the continuous nightly thunderstorms and wondered where I would wake up the next morning should God decide my hotel room was a trailer park.

My most unusual memory of Tusla is a small bar which, I was introduced to by the cast and director. The main point of interest hung over the bar itself. About ten feet off the ground was an absolutely huge moose head complete with an impressive array of antlers. That is not the interesting part of this story. The attraction of that bar hung from the antlers. Over the years, the owner managed to accumulate a collection of ... easily... possibly... over 200 bras that were now draped over the unfortunate moose. I suppose you could say that the moose had a nice rack.

It's the bar policy that if you donate your bra to the collection, you get to drink free that night. There were red, yellow, blue, pink, ivory and black ones. The owner told me he takes them down at least twice a year to wash them, to keep the dust from staining them. He also mentioned to me that occasionally, a very hung over woman would limp into the bar the next day to beg for her bra back, often saying that it was a very expensive bra. But there is a no return policy at this bar unless they return the alcohol. (I must remember to institute this rule at my dinner parties.)

And a few months later, I was invited to a theatre workshop in Wisconsin, compliments of that Tulsa director who lived in Wisconsin. While there, she and the cast of the play we were working on decided to hold what they called a "Canadian Party" in my honour. This mainly consisted of sitting around drinking some American Labatt's Blue, eating doughnuts from a Dunkin' Doughnuts and watching a video of the Mackenzie Brother's movie "Strange Brew". They even had a bottle of Canadian Club Whiskey out for me. It was almost like being at home, although I refused to wear the mandatory toque handed to me. That was basically the extent of their knowledge of Canada. Well that, plus hockey and Pamela Anderson.

Americans... you just gotta love them.

In my travels, numerous expatriate Canadians enthusiastically introduced themselves to me. It wasn't long before we found ourselves pining for those unique Canadian experiences completely unavailable in the mighty United States. If I had a nickel (American, not Canadian) for every ex-Canadian that asked me how I survive with no vinegar on my French fries; if I managed to smuggle any butter tarts across the border; if I remembered how to make that singularly Canadian drink known as a Caesar (which if you try to describe the recipe to a Yankee bartender they look at you like you're crazy); or, if I had a spare Stompin' Tom CD on me. It's truly sad and pathetic to witness.

But if you really want to throw Americans into a state of confusion, take it from personal experience, just casually tell them two things. Firstly, that you vacation regularly in Cuba. I have stopped many dinner conversations by letting that small migratory fact nonchalantly slip out while in a country where travel to the tiny communist country is illegal. They react like you've been to Mars.

Secondly, tell them you're from Toronto (even if you're not) where the two largest landmarks are the world's biggest phallic symbol –the CN Tower, which is right beside what appears to be an absolutely huge boob –the Skydome. That will make them wonder about Canadians.

On The Road Again
(things I've seen and a few I shouldn't have)

BANGING ON THE DOOR

Now I'm a traveling kind of guy; I've been to a lot of places; seen a lot of wonderful lands; and had my share of unique adventures. But this was a first for me. Picture it. I'm on my way to Vermont for a series of dramaturgical (theatre stuff) meetings with the Artistic Director of an American theatre company interested in producing one of my plays. During the summer the A.D. teaches a course in Theatre at a college in Vermont. He wants to meet me. So like the mountain and Mohammed, I was willing to go if he provided the way. With a plane ticket in hand for a flight on Wednesday, I was busy packing my bags on a Tuesday when the call came in.

It was the A.D.'s executive assistant. There was a wrinkle in the plans. I was the wrinkle. Or more accurately, Toronto was the wrinkle. The college campus told the executive assistant that upon arrival, I would have to sign a document stating I had not visited any cities on the Centre for Disease Control's (CDC) list of SARS hot spots. The Executive Assistant struggled to find the correct words to tell this woman but she found them.

"He's flying in from Toronto. He lives in Toronto." I'm told there was a slight pause on the other end, then a polite ("Well I'm sorry, but he won't be allowed on Campus,") refusal. Now keep in mind, this was a good week after Toronto was taken off the World Health Organization's list of hot spots. But this college Campus follows the edicts of the CDC which had not, and was rather inflexible on the subject. I was not allowed to enter their hallowed halls of education. I had visions of my first great American production going up in smoke... there goes that Pulitzer; that Tony; that Nobel literature award thingee.

As a starving playwright and professional humourist, for some reason whenever the harsh hand of reality slaps me in the face, God's always make sure it's wearing a glove of irony. At least that way, it makes the sting more interesting.

For instance, was I the only one who saw the irony, the peculiar twist of historical fate, in that I, a person of Aboriginal ancestry, was not being allowed into a country because of the fear of a disease?! Where was this belief five hundred years ago! That's like saying I wouldn't be allowed to phone a telemarketer because I just might annoy them. I was stunned. Part of me (the Trickster part) was tempted to go down to Vermont, and take a casual walk around the campus wearing a shirt that proudly boasted the name Toronto on it, and occasionally, cough. Every few minutes, whereever I would be on my journey across the campus, I would extol the virtues of the CN Tower or the Skydome or our subway system, then let out an increasingly harsh cough where ever I went. It would have been a defeatist act but it sure would have been fun.

How's this for the right hand doesn't know what the left hand is doing. This theatre company that was in danger of losing the cost of a plane ticket from a sudden cancellation, started arguing with the airlines. They wanted a better refund because it was not their fault I couldn't use the ticket, it was the campus and the CDC who nullified the situation. Meanwhile, the airline's response was, "We take our direction from the World Health Organization. And they say it's okay to travel to and from Toronto. No refund."

So there I was, hoping and expecting to bring the glory and genius of Native theatre to America but stopped by a disease I didn't have. A disease that nobody I knew had. By a people that didn't have the disease. I think they're still pissed off we didn't support them in the Iraqi war. Yet, if memory serves me correctly, the Americans are not quite fully convinced there's officially such a thing as the Persian Gulf Syndrome.

I have a few more trips planned to the States in the next few months and now I'm beginning to get a little concerned about what America will fear next from me and other Torontonians. Mad Cow Disease... Albertans beware. The West Nile Virus... I think that's already made it's way into the States. I just hope they don't find out about the great Crabs epidemic of 1999, one of the less reported afflictions. I was not a victim then but, then again, I wasn't a victim of SARS either.

The final insult, the final ironic kick to the kidney, happened that next morning –the Wednesday morning I was scheduled to leave for the lovely state of Vermont. As I morosely unpacked and listened to the Radio, the CBC announced that the Centre for Disease Control in Atlanta had just lifted its Toronto travel warning. It was now safe to migrate. If I had taken my flight like I had planned, it all would have been a moot point.

I hate when stuff like that happens.

MY EUROPEAN POW WOW

When Europeans first landed on these shores so many years ago, it was estimated there were approximately 100 million Native people waiting here to welcome them with local delicacies like tomatoes, potatoes, tobacco and corn. In the intervening five hundred plus years, our effects on the land across the big pond known as the Atlantic is often thought of being limited to produce, canoes and kayaks. Imagine my surprise when I found myself in Italy, at the Turin International Book Fair on what turned out to be a positively Indigenous travel experience. Since Canada was a featured exhibit at the Fair, I was one of twenty-one Canadian authors (with a heavy focus of Italian-Canadian writers) invited to introduce Italians to the wonders of Canadian literature. Nino Ricci bought me a cappaccino. Steven Heighton, Jeffrey Moore and I gossiped about our lovely writer wrangler. John Ralston Saul asked what one of my books was about. I asked Canada's resident philosopher, "John, what's it ALL about?"

As usual, I was the only First Nations author at the Fair and the only writer not translated into Italian. Evidently Native theatre and humour are not of particular interest in the land of Columbus and Cabot (born Coboto in Venice). I was there for colour. Or so I thought. During the seven days I spent in Italy, I was absolutely overwhelmed by the amount of intentional and surprisingly random amounts of Aboriginal influence and representation in Turin. At the Book Fair itself, home to three huge venues of publishers exhibits amounting to thousands of different Italian books for every taste, I found one book titled *Guida alle Riserve Indinae di Stati Uniti E Canada*, It was a guide to every Native community in North America. While I doubt it was a best seller, it was still a shock. I'd expect this from the Germans, not the Italians.

One night I was asked to attend a book launching, of an Italian translation of a Canadian book. I was shocked to discover it was *Racconti Eroti Ci Degli Indiani Canadesi*, better known to thousands of Native readers across Canada as *Tales From The Smokehouse*. This book is a collection of supposedly Native erotic tales compiled by a not so Indigenous sounding gentleman named Herbert T. Schwarz and published way back in 1974. Its pedigree as a respectable source of authentic legends is suspect though, since one of the "tales" takes place during the 1967 Montreal Expo. During the launch, an Italian anthropologist delivered a quick lecture on the nature of First Nations erotic storytelling. I sure wish I could have understood the man. It sounded interesting. Then, a professional storyteller proceeded to read one of the tales. Again, it sounded interesting. I had read the book many years ago, but it sure looked and sounded different in Italian.

The book was translated and published by an organization called Soconal Incomindios, a non-profit organization whose goal is "to unite all those who are interested in the Aboriginal Peoples of the Americas –in their cultures, as well as in their various political, social and cultural conditions." Located in downtown Turin, they even have their own magazine called *TEPEE: Comitato Di Solidarieta Con Popoli Nativi Americani* which has been around since 1984. In the current issue, No. 28, topics explored include *"Culture Native Ed Ecosistema"* and *"Philippe Jacquin, L'Indiano Bianco Dell'Universita` Francese."*

A few nights later, Soconal Incomindios presented a reading by Lakota poet Gilbert Douville, originally from Rosebud, South Dakota, and now living in Turin via an Italian wife he met while on tour with an American Native dance troupe. When not writing poems, Douville makes jewelry and ironically, teaches English as a second language. Evidently I was not the only moccasin on the "boot." (Italy)

More surprising, a week prior to the Book Fair the Universita` Degli Studi Di Torino invited me to a conference titled *INDIAN STORIES INDIAN HISTORIES: Storia e Storie degli Indiani d'America*; but due to other reasons I was unable to attend. It looked like a fascinating conference with topics such as "Framing the Text: Bill Miller, Buffy Ste. Marie and Modern Native Visualisation Imagery," "Trickster Shift:Art and Literature (from the University of Helsinki?!), "Contemporary Tales among Cree and Blackfeet" and "The Early Collecting Practice of the Museum of Anthropology at the University of British Columbia." I'm glad I missed that last one.

My European journey got stranger and stranger. After the book launch of the Italian/Aboriginal erotic tales, a young Turin lady drove me back to my hotel. Along the way we chatted. I asked if she was a student. With her makeshift English and a thick accent, she managed to convey that she got her degree in Native Studies last year. I wanted to make sure I understood her correctly but indeed, she got her degree in Native Studies. In Italy. I guess that proves the saying that anything is truly possible.

On a walking tour of Turin, I was further inclined to wonder if these awesome adventures were some sort of practical joke. Too many things were proving to be a tad too coincidental for your average Native tourist to believe. Our tour guide told us that before Italy had consolidated into the present country we all know and love, it was a collection of city states. Turin was a particularly important one. It was run by the House of Savoy which has a close connection to the French Crown. As a sign of solidarity and support, the city of Turin sent 1200 of their best soldiers in 1666 to Quebec to help the French fight the Iroquois. Eight hundred returned home as several hundred elected to stay behind in this new country, which explains why there are so many French Canadians with Italian last names. Also, local fable has it the soldiers brought back an unknown number of people of an Aboriginal nature who were curious to see the strange new world where all these strange folks had come from. They ended up settling down and being absorbed into the population. They soon disappeared into legend. I suppose that's why so many Italians have dark complexions and even darker hair. You think? These first Italian/Indian Métis today are affectionately known, (politically incorrectly), as Awopahos.

Several years later, when the new palace for the House of Savoy was being built, the architect wanted to honour those soldiers who went off to battle the savages. Above all the first floor windows in the new palace, are large brick images of Native people designed by an architect who had never been out of Europe. There are eight of them in a row; all with four brick feathers standing straight up. They sadly smile down at the Turins as if to say, "I only came for the Gelato."

The best and most indicative observation to top off this surreal trip happened on the way to the airport. When the taxi stopped at a red light, I gazed out the window, pondering transcontinental Native thoughts. In the car right next to us, was a small Fiat with a dreamcatcher hanging on the rearview mirror.

Why did I bother leaving Canada?

THINGS YOU LEARN IN L.A.

Recently, I just got back from L.A. (I love saying that) where *The Buz'gem Blues* opened (I love saying that too). While there, I learned NBC finally shot what they call "a showcase of a pilot" for an Aboriginal sitcom a few months ago. For several years, NBC was shaking the bushes looking for talented Native comedians and writers to do something like this. Well, they finally put their money where their mouth is. Unfortunately, they chose the most predictable Native plot currently available in North American pop culture.

As I was told, the half hour sitcom called *Blood Brothers* revolves around a small impoverished Reservation somewhere in the American heartland being courted by a huge company interested in turning their bingo hall into a huge casino and all the traditional (no pun intended) hilarious hijinks that soon ensue. Practically every time I see Native people on American television, it's usually in relation to casinos and gambling in some form. I remember when television representation consisted largely of alcoholism and working high steel. Boy, have we come far.

Anyone familiar with the television industry knows there's little chance of this show becoming a series. The death rate of television pilots is equivalent to the chances of electing a First Nations person as leader of the Alliance party of Canada, or a First Nations person even wanting to be elected leader of the Alliance Party of Canada –slim to none. The usual ratio is five pilots picked for every hundred or so produced. Don't expect to see Blood Brothers on the fall schedule.

While I applaud NBC and its first foray into Native humour, I am a little disgruntled with their topic matter. As someone who travels extensively visiting rural and urban Native communities across North America on a continuous basis, I know that Aboriginal life is incredibly funny and there are a hundreds of incredibly original funny stories happening every day. It's a pity NBC didn't tap into that unique reservoir of life and do something a little more innovative.

Case in point, one of the Native actors in my play told me a very humorous story about visiting his in-laws. While there, his in-laws invited him out on the lake, to experience the unique sport of ice fishing. For those not familiar with the sport, little shacks the size of an outhouse dot frozen lakes while men (and occasionally women) sit around holes cut in the ice and fish. More often than not, it's a bonding experience with a pickerel dinner payoff. For some, it's a chance to enjoy the solitude. Evidently this was an exceptional experience for this Native actor for a number of reasons. First of all, he's Pueblo-Apache andhis territory in the American southwest is not known for its lakes, let alone frozen ones. Perhaps a little more unusual was when his in-laws suggested he should have been out ice fishing a week earlier when the ice shack hookers came around.

I don't know that much about the sex trade, but it seems to me that ice shack hookers must be at the low end of the hooker spectrum. What can you do in a ski-doo suit surrounded by worms? Can you pay them in fish? I wonder what you can get for three bass and a perch? (Am I incredibly naive to be asking these questions?)

While this story might not make for a family oriented or culturally sensitive television show about North America's Indigenous people, it would be a lot more interesting than yet another tale of Native casinos. Stories like his is an example of the funny yet different things that happen in a Native community. But what do I know. The way Canadian television industry is today there is little chance of us doing our own shows. Instead we watch CBC news to be filled in on the dysfunctional Aboriginal story of the day. Or we can watch APTN and learn how to gut a seal, caribou, deer, arctic char or elk (each day of the week seems to have an animal gutting lesson).

In L.A, I found that vegetarians have very little sense of humour. I was hanging out with some L.A. people, when I was asked if we had PETA in Canada. PETA stands for the People for the Ethical Treatment of Animals but I commented that yes, I was a card-carrying member of PETA –People who Eat Tasty Animals. I barely got out of California intact. They almost ate me alive.

A CANADIAN INDIAN ABROAD

Being a Canadian, especially a Torontonian, who travels this complex world has become increasingly more interesting, through no great effort of my own. Recently, I was fortunate to attend a conference on humour in Dijon, France where I lectured on the wonders of the Aboriginal funny bone. Having traveled quite a bit, there is a set routine many of us travelers go through. After landing in Paris, just before boarding the train to Dijon, I scoured a news stand looking for something in English to read on the long train ride. Long ago, I gave up expecting to find a Canadian paper or magazine in Europe, so I've had to be content with getting news filtered through the American Press. I speak of USA Today, whose distribution usually blankets most of Europe.

I went to four newsstands in the airport and three at the train station. This newspaper did not seem to exist. I thought, maybe they were sold out. I looked for it in Dijon over the next three days and on my return to the Paris train station on my way to Belgium. I didn't find it in Brussels, the French speaking capital. Or when I returned a few days later to the Paris Airport to come home. Seven days in France and Belgium and no sign of an American newspaper. While I'm not a particularly avid fan of the paper, it is nice to read what's happening in North America. Such an obvious absence of USA Today made me wonder if this was a reaction, or a statement in support of France's reluctance to participate in the war in Iraq? Were they boycotting the paper? This possibility made me dig deep into my suitcase and place a number of Canadian flag pins all over my luggage and jacket. My dialogue was punctuated with far more *eh's* than I normally would.

As I boarded an Air Canada plane for the return home, I became aware of a nagging pain in my throat and sinuses. Somewhere in my travels, I had picked up a cold instead of USA Today. I sought solace in the fact it wasn't just a common cold but an exotic French cold. In my misery all the way home, I found myself going "le cough" and "la sneeze" and realized I had learned more French from Pepe LePew than my grade five French teacher, Madame Whitney. As I "le sniffled", the flight attendant gave me a gift from Heaven, a Globe and Mail. I quickly scanned it for news and my eyes caught the screaming headline "SARS EPIDEMIC FEARED"... that was my introduction back into Canadian life. While I'd been away, Severe Acute Respiratory Syndrome (SARS) had taken Canada by storm. That and Air Canada, the company whose plane I was hoping would soon take off, was going broke. Welcome home, Drew.

Back in Canada, I remember heading through customs, le coughing and le sniffling. Oddly enough, I practically had a whole line to myself. Thank heavens for small mercies. I made it home late that night, and was up early the next morning for yet another trip, this time to Saskatoon. Now there's culture shock. Paris, Dijon and Brussels, then Saskatoon. I was scheduled to hold two workshops at an Aboriginal Education conference there.

The paranoia in Toronto and throughout the country was quite evident during that part of my journey. At the airport, I checked in, grabbed a coffee, all the time la sneezing, la blowing nose, la watery eyes. People were watching me closely and staying further away than normal in the cramped airport. I could actually see people around me on the plane giving me the evil eye. The poor woman beside me was leaning halfway into the aisle. It was on that flight that I discovered, again in the Globe and Mail, that Australia had urged its people not to visit the fair city of Toronto, believed to be a centre for the SARS disease. Charming, I thought, as I continued to le hack my lungs out. Saskatoon continued the sense of alienation and apprehension. I was from Toronto and I was obviously sick. I wanted to yell out that, like any good First Nations person, I had gotten my virus from Europe, not China. Unfortunately, we already have a five hundred year history of that. One shining note in this sad tale is that the people at the conference were very nice and not so paranoid. In a twenty-four hour period, at least two dozen people said to me with a conspiratorial grin as I le coughed, "Maybe you've got SARS." Maybe because I work with humour but it amazes me how many individuals believe they are the first one to make a joke like that. Also, with my first name being Drew, I can't tell you how many people have asked me if I was related to Nancy Drew, or "did Drew drew a picture?" Trust me, if you've thought of it, so have at least two hundred other people. Same with the SARS joke. I politely smiled and le blew my nose.

Today, the exotic French cold is gone, but SARS and the war (and/or its remnants) remain. Next month, I have a trip planned to Italy. I may or may not be able to find a copy of USA Today. In the big picture of life, it's not all that important. If I happen to come down with a cold, maybe I won't be so annoyed, considering all the other more newsworthy afflictions in the world news.

EVERYTHING A NATIVE PERSON NEEDS TO KNOW
ABOUT VISITING GERMANY

Germany is an ancient country, one locked in complex tradition and memory. Its people, who were tribal in the days of the Roman empire, now bask in a culinary world of breads, sausages and beer. Actually, they are not that different from most Native communities. Within their Teutonic culture are many societal nuances and behavioral practices that might befuddle your average Aboriginal traveler, should they find themselves in that central European country. As a frequent visitor to Germany, I have taken the liberty of putting together an Aboriginal tourist guide book. Essentially, a primer or travel book for overseas Indigenous travelers (and various other cultures should they be interested) to make the journey less stressful and more interesting. The guide book contains references to the many personal observations and adventures from my travels along the Baltic, up and down the Rhine, across Bavaria, and an occasional foray into the former East Germany. With a little advance knowledge, any trip to Germany can be fun filled and exciting.

The first thing to know is they do not accept Canadian Tire money no matter how hard you try. Nor do they understand the concept of a Status Card and not paying taxes. Even when you say it in German!

Depending on your personal preferences when it comes to drinking wine, do not be alarmed if they offer you a bottle of wine with a screw top lid. There are issues in Germany dealing with the use of cork and the potential damage it is doing to the environment and the cork trees. Many have turned to plastic corks while others now use a twist top. However, do resist the urge to drink it out of a brown paper bag. Some etiquette rules never change.

When you see signs posted saying 'ausfahrt', do not do what you think it is asking, it is merely a traffic sign saying 'exit'.

Some small hotels do not provide soap in the bathrooms. You are expected to bring your own. As a result, do not underestimate the washing capabilities of shampoo or, if desperate enough, toothpaste. Your armpits will be minty fresh and cavity free.

If you are lucky enough to visit the small Bavarian town of Erlengen during the spring Asparagus Festival, and if you look hard enough, you will find a local delicacy-asparagus ice cream. Don't worry. It's not the North American green variety, but the tasty white variety, which I'm sure makes it all the more palatable. This way you can tell your mother you ate all your vegetables.

For those who are shy by nature, try to avoid the public washroom at the Stuttgart train station which require a fee of .20 Euros to use. If you don't have exact change, there is a glass booth located (a scant fifteen feet) across from the urinals, where an older, disapproving woman sits surveying her domain, watching the waterworks, and doling out change. Those who suffer from performance anxiety might want to seek other avenues of relief. Oddly enough, as I exited the said washroom, she shook her head in what seemed to be pity and handed me back my .20 Euros.

If you suffer from jet lag, don't be surprised to find yourself wandering about your room at 3:00 a.m. wondering what to do until breakfast. Be less surprised if, you turn the television on, and see a television show broadcast all night, featuring nothing but female strippers, for five and a half hours... or so I was told.

If you're lucky, you might be taken for a ride in one of the new computerized cars. Everything is automatic, including a display screen on the dashboard that features maps, driving coordinates, a compass, temperature and other cool instrumentation. Instead of a key, you use a plastic card that slides into a slot and starts the car automatically. Just imagine that car sitting derelict on your front lawn!

Motorcycles in Germany have taken a quantum leap ahead. There is one model currently driving up and down the Autobahn that is touted as eliminating the need for a crash helmet. In an accident, the designers have built into the frame the equivalent of a roll bar. It is attached at the rear of the machine, extending in a forward half-circle to meet the handlebars and windshield. Not only that, the seat includes a seat belt. Darn clever, those Germans.

If you want to get on the German people's good side, wear your standard ribbon shirt; but make sure the ribbon's match the German national colors of black, gold and red. Tell them you planned that all along (even though you bought the shirt at a Pow wow on Manitoulin Island in 1989), in honour of the Berlin Wall coming down. Tell them it is your way of demonstrating solidarity with them and that your heart will always be with the German people... a kind of like "Polka With Wolves" scenario.

Beware of cities like Munich, where at the local beer garden (there are hundreds in the city, some seating as many as 1,300) people suggest you have a "couple of beers" with them. If you are friendly and no stranger to beer, you might order such a liquid. Don't be too shocked when the waitress brings you a LITRE stein and four days later you wake up in Finland trying to teach Laplanders how to play bingo.

YOU CAN TAKE THE BOY OUT OF THE REZ...

One of the things I always pride myself on is that I tend to look at the world with the wide-eyed innocence which I believe comes from growing up on my Ojibway Reserve. In the years since I left those weed-choked shores of my childhood, I've had the opportunity to travel around the world, see amazing things, and meet fascinating people. Yet, wherever I am I still find within a sense of enthusiasm and child-like joy with the world. I reflect much of it in my writing.

I just got back from a week in Los Angeles and Burbank, California. Boy. What an adventure! I was there for a production workshop of my new comedy play titled The Buz'Gem Blues, which provided me with an opportunity to hang out in the outskirts of Hollywood. I knew I was near that area because my cab kept driving past production studios for ABC, NBC, Disney, the Cartoon Network, and BET (Black Entertainment Television). It's no secret that Burbank/Hollywood is primarily an industry town, slightly different than a pulp and paper mill town like Prince George or Espanola. Okay, maybe a lot different. The populace's devotion to their industry is amazing. I went shopping in a used book store, and I immediately noticed one whole wall devoted to bound movie scripts that were for sale. I'm not talking about professionally published scripts or books you might find at Chapters. These were production scripts, made up of loosely bound white paper. I pondered this as I took a cab to work, wondering about the influence film and television had in this town. As we drove past the Church of Scientolgy Celebrity Centre, I thought about towns like London, the insurance capital of Canada, and Oshawa our own motor city. Did they have this same allegiance to their industry? I dismissed that idea as we drove by an overpass with some graffiti art. It took me a second to realize it was a remarkably accurate portrait of a young Tony Curtis circa Some Like It Hot.

We drove by the Bette Davis Park, parked at the Mary Pickford Education Centre and I made my way to the Gene Autry Western Heritage Museum where we were rehearsing. The irony was not lost upon me. That night we all hung out in the hotel kareoke bar called the Casting Call Lounge.

My most unusual observation came from a magazine I picked up to read at breakfast, called the L.A. WEEKLY. It seemed a typical arts

61

and politics weekly. The cover story was about a Mexican film going global. I opened up the magazine and found an ad for an institute called "New Me" which was advertising breast augmentation for $2899.00. That is American dollars. If the disproportionate exchange rate holds up, does that mean American breasts are 44% larger? Wow! You do get more for your money down there. "New Me" also advertised liposuction, face-lifts, nasal resculpturing, something called a browlift, and lip augmentation was a steal at $999.00. The back cover really got my attention. Another surgical institute was offering much the same except for a few "extras". What caught my eye was their specialties, male and female breast reduction, vaginal tightening, and, my favorite, labial reduction. I suppose this can be filed in the "What to get the person who has everything" file.

Perhaps the most exciting part of my journey was meeting someone famous, What's a trip to L.A. without a sighting? During the reading of my play when I noticed this pretty woman in the crowd. She looked familiar but I couldn't place her; and it bothered me. I only knew three people in L.A., two of whom were producing this workshop for a Native (or rather "Indian" as they say in the States) theatre festival called Native Voices, and the other was an ex-girlfriend. Unless she had gotten an awful lot of that plastic surgery stuff., this wasn't her.

Maybe I knew this woman from film or television. Then it hit me. Jennifer Tilly, star of *Bullets Over Broadway*, *Bride of Chucky*, *Bound* and *Shadow Of The Wolf*, was in the audience. Even more spectacular, we were introduced after the reading and got to casually chatting. She mentioned that growing up in British Columbia her mother always told her their family had some Native blood. "What Nation or Tribe?" I asked.

She replied "Ojibway. Ever heard of them?"

I just about swallowed my tongue. Most people in the States who claim Native blood are either Cherokee, Choctaw, or Lakota. Occasionally you'll find an Iroquois, but an Ojibway in L.A. is rare. I remember a legend of sorts from my childhood, that tells of a vanload of people driving down from the mighty island of Manitoulin on their way to a sacred Vancouver Canucks game. They ran out of gas money somewhere near New Westminster and couldn't return home. They decided to stay in B.C. And the legend grew. So this is what happened to them! The lovely Ms Tilly is still researching her origins but anyone as cute as she is has to have some Ojibway blood flowing in them.

The next morning at 6:30 a.m., I was at the airport waiting for a flight home and watching people in the bar have their morning Bloody Mary. I took stock of my trip and knew, it was definitely worth writing about. One thing kept bothering me. Should I have offered to teach Jennifer Tilly the secret Ojibway handshake?

Rez Politics
(WHO'S DOING WHAT TO WHO, HOW OFTEN, AND FOR HOW MUCH)

THROWING MY HEADBAND INTO THE RING

On July 16, somewhere deep in the bowels of Edmonton, the future of Canada's status Aboriginal people will be decided. The election of the Grand Chief of the Assembly of First Nation (AFN), Canada's leading first Nations political and advocacy group, is proving to be one of the most contentious in recent history. Facing each other across the election floor will be incumbent Grand Chief Matthew Coon Come, former Grand Chief Phil Fontaine, and challenger Six Nations Chief Roberta Jamieson (one of the few woman to run for the office but the first to be a real contender for the position).

Several provocative issues make this election a most pivotal one in recent Aboriginal history. The controversy surrounding the universal opposition to First Nations Governance Act (FNGA's) Bill C-7, and the best way for the AFN to deal with the Federal Government, to negotiate, litigate or demonstrate, or all three. The grassroots issue of exploring the possibility that all Status Indians have a vote in the election, not only the Chiefs of the 633 bands which AFN represents. All these issues have made the 24th Annual AGA one to watch.

I feel it is my duty as a proud, card-carrying Native person interested in doing my bit for the people to officially declare my candidacy for the office of Grand Chief. Granted, the deadline for nominations ended on June 11, but I am counting on a strong write-in campaign to bring my message to people in all four directions. I have no political background, never went to University, never held any type of office and have voted only once in my life (because my girlfriend of the time made it quite clear the NDP ruled her ethics, heart, and other parts of her body). It's hard to counterpoint an argument like that. I am going to plan my whole campaign upon my election slogan. Imagine a picture of yours truly and underneath it, printed in bright red letters, "You Could Do Worse."

That being said, if I am going to succeed in nailing this $125,000 a year job, I will need more than just a pithy catch phrase. I will also need a platform, and to take a position on the relevant issues. It seems to be a foregone conclusion that FNGA is universally disliked. Most candidates believe it is fundamentally flawed because it is built upon the Indian act and introduces even more legislation, rules and regulations to First Nations. The FNGA strengthens the Ministers power and gives him new powers over First Nations, thus giving the Federal government yet more control over Aboriginal lives.

Politically aware First Nations people think the Indian Act should be put aside and any legislation if required, should build on Section 35 of the 1982 Constitution Act which recognizes inherent Aboriginal and Treaty rights. This would call for a Treaty-making and implementation process dealing with lands and resource issues and real self-government at the national level. As an official candidate, I say that FNGA should stand for "For Now, Go Away."

There is criticism of how the AFN's profile in Ottawa has lapsed in recent years. Mr. Fontaine thinks it has been reduced to "a protest organization." Ovide Mercredi, the former Grand Chief, had a highly publicized confrontational and antagonistic relationship Minister of Indian Affairs, Ron Irwin. Rumour is, it got to the point where the Minister refused to take the Mercredi's phone calls. As a result, communication between the two organizations aimed at improving the lives of Canada's Native people suffered an all time low.

I blame it on suits. Throughout history, wars have been started, lands swindled, Residential schools planned, and other atrocities in history (Aboriginal or not) have been orchestrated by people wearing suits in one form or another. I think the monochromatic colour scheme of suits, tight collar buttons and ties restrict blood to the brain and encourages aggression and confrontation. I'll bet David Ahenekew was wearing a suit when he said those anti-Semitic remarks.

Yes, I know the argument. Suits don't hurt people, people hurt people. Still, it does seem awfully suspicious. Anytime a Native person goes to jail, and raises the already incredibly high Aboriginal incarceration rate, there's always a couple of suits nearby. People who took our kids away for adoption, in suits. Government officials saying our tax free status is questionable, in suits. Oil executive that were harassing the Lubicon Lake people for their natural resources, in suits. People at the Canada Council who denied me my last grant, in suits. There is a definite theme here. I do own a couple of suits myself; but I only wear them for self-defence.

Upon my election, the first thing I would do is ban the wearing of suits at any organizational function, meeting or conference of the AFN. Historically, I feel suits promote a confrontational attitude. So, I would hold all official gatherings, meetings and sessions in a hot tub. It is my experience that it can be quite difficult to get adversarial while in a hot tub. Everybody is laid back, comfortable, enjoying the hot water, and much more agreeable in nature. I definitely feel more could be accomplished through hot tub negotiations than by wearing a tie. It's a radical alternative to present First Nations and government relations, and would make all those official discussions and dialogues a little more interesting. The practice might even catch on. Imagine a First Ministers Conference with John Chretien, Ralph Klein and Ernie Eves in a hot tub...then again, maybe you shouldn't.

There is so much more to the job, but a candidate needs to start somewhere. Every journey starts with a first step. If the Liberals can have a Red Book, so can the Aboriginal Nation, except ours will be white... just for irony's sake. What's politics without some form of irony.

ART AND THE REGULAR INDIAN

I have a very good friend who has gone to great pains to inform me of two startling facts about the average Native community that I was unaware of. First of all, the university degree she earned many winters back has allowed her the educated insight to break the Aboriginal population of Canada down into two categories with-its and regular Annishnawbe (Ljibway).. Secondly, *regular* Annishnawbe have the only true understanding and appreciation that can be considered legitimate forms of aboriginal artistic expression. *With-its* are Aboriginal artists doing what they do because they have been corrupted by the dominant society. This concept made me re-evaluate my career.

Perhaps an explanation is in order. We were having a discussion about a project I'm working on (a documentary on Native Erotica) and how I'd spent the last eighteen months researching the reclaiming of aboriginal sexuality. The discussion derived her belief that there is no such thing as Native Erotica (which may or may not be true). I told her that celebrated poet Kateri Akiwenzie-Damm was in the final throes of putting together a book on First Nations literary erotica, so evidently some people in the community were talking about it.

My friend completely dismissed both projects saying they were of complete non-interest to *regular* Indians on the reserve because erotica wasn't part of our everyday life. She argued that *regular* Indians on the reserve didn't care about things like that; it's something they wouldn't discuss; it was an influence introduced by the European culture; and those who participated in avenues of exploration *like that* had capitulated to the dominant culture. *With-its* were just playing into their game. *Regular Indians* wouldn't buy Kateri's erotica book or see my documentary but White people would... maybe *with-it* Indians too. She wanted to know who had asked me to do this film.

"The National Film Board of Canada. I worked with one of the executive producers at the Toronto office."

She asked me if it was a White woman.

"Yes, a White woman," I responded.

She said something like, "Well, there you go," as if she'd won some big victory, Then proclaimed, "A *White* woman wants you to do a documentary on *Native* erotica."

I pointed out that I had suggested the topic, researched it and if the funding came through, I would direct it too. I told her I got the idea after seeing an art show called EXPOSED, a collection of erotic Native visual and installation art, curated by Native people, which toured the country. That's about the time the term *with-its* was introduced.

"These are not things *regular* Indians would be interested in," she said. "Only, I guess those you'd call *with-its*. I don't think you should do the documentary. You're only contributing to the artistic desires of White people."

As she talked, I looked around the room admiring at least a dozen stunningly beautiful quilts which she had created scattered throughout her home. I wanted to comment that I hadn't seen any quilts or quilt-like images on any of the pictographs or petroglyphs seen on my travels; but, I thought the better of it.

The people who had put together the erotic art show had had similar concerns about their project. Not wanting to be disrespectful, they consulted an Elder in southern Saskatchewan who congratulated them on the project and said that it was about time someone reclaimed our sexuality. To which my friend commented, "How do you know she was a real Elder? Could she have been an Elder of convenience?" Now it was my turn to enter the discussion with more than a "but...," "I...," "You don't...,"

"As a playwright, film maker, television writer, no one is more aware than me of the changing face of Aboriginal society. I've had eighteen years on the Reserve and twenty-two in the urban environment. I've visited at least a 120 Native communities across Canada and the United States. Suffice it to say I have some experience with nearly all aspects of the Native community. It has often been said that we have gone from telling stories around the campfire to telling stories on the stage or television. People change. The Ojibway spoken by my mother is no doubt different than that spoken by her grandparents and their grandparents. Cultures are evolving. Constantly."

"Exactly," my friend said. "But what is making it happen?"

"The environment."

She nodded, "And what's evolving our culture today?"

Taking a wild guess, I answered "The 21st Century."

"Exactly. White influences."

I couldn't help but think how this implied that Native people have no noticeable influence in the 21st Century (which I found kind of depressing, if not defeatist).

Then she added, "Not our ways."

"So you aren't really comfortable living in this split level house with heating and plumbing?" I said.

It was here she got really upset.

"I resent you for asking me a question like that. That's the kind of question a White person would ask."

I was tempted to point out I am half White but, she knew that already. Come to think of it, she is half White too.

"It's a stupid question. Where else do you expect me to live? Would you expect me to go back and live in a shack?"

I was puzzled. "Traditionally, I never heard of Native people living in shacks."

"Now you're just arguing." With a wave of her hand she dismissed me, abruptly ending our conversation.

Granted, my seventy-one-year-old mother whose first language is Ojibway and as Native as they come probably wouldn't be interested in a book or documentary on Native erotica. But, I can guarantee a few uncles might hazard a peek. This kind of generalization does a great disservice to the *regular* Annishnawbe. In my travels I have met many Reserve Indians who have a legitimate interest in non-Reserve issues and the arts. I should also mention that conversation with my friend happened over a glass of traditional California Chardonnay, which not long after, she had finished watching *regular* soap operas on *regular* television.

But I will admit I am in true awe of my friend. It is seldom that you meet somebody who has the authority to speak for an entire population of people and can categorically maintain what they will or won't be interested in, and ironically with utter confidence. Perhaps she should get a job in marketing.

Oh well, what do I know? I'm just a *with-it*, not a *regular* Annishnawbe. Evidently, somewhere along the Pow Wow trail I went from being a Reserve Indian to an Urban Indian to an Urbane Indian.

SOMETIMES LIFE IS JUST TOO INTERESTING – 2003

I read in a book that one of the blessings a person can bestow upon you will be either a good benediction or bad one depending on how it pans out. "May you live in interesting times." This sounds innocuous enough, but during the past few months, within the Native community, there seems to be nothing but interesting times to live through. To tell you the truth, I'm sure many skins across this country wish things weren't so darn interesting. I am talking about the controversial things that seem to be enveloping our communities. Native people and their issues have been propping up on the evening news far too often. Sometimes, it's like *The National* is actually APTN'S *In Vision News*.

The less said about the whole David Ahenekew mess and its effects on Judeo –Aboriginal relations the better. A well-respected man, who many viewed as the voice of the Saskatchewan Native, has ended his time in the public eye in disgrace. For those that don't remember this disgraceful debacle, David Ahenekew told a reporter that Hitler was doing a good thing when he tried to wipe out the Jews during World War II. However, we should be grateful for small miracles. Few men could better demonstrate the difference between a cranky old man and an Elder. I agree with those who say a lifetime of hard work and selfless achievement should not immediately be dismissed because of one stupid mistake, however enormous. Maybe he forgot his eagle feather at home that day.

Also of recent newsworthy discussion is that old argument dealing with who is and isn't Métis. Yet another Indigenous definition to deal with. Are the true inheritors of that proud race those with ancestral and blood connections to Louis Riel (whom I'm told was only an eighth Native) or Gabriel Dumont? Or can it refer to anyone of mixed blood? Nearly every province in Canada has a Métis association now. I don't think the Battle of Batoche was waged that far afield. The Métis identity is a testy subject. On one hand, you have those with a historical and geographical connection to the Métis name. On the other hand, the terms mixed-blood, half-breed and non-Status Indian are so unromantic. My answer... those with specific prairie lineage be called Riel Métis and all the rest will be called Real Métis. Phonetically, they sound almost identical.

Within the last month, there's been a lot of publicity about the latest national census. The population of Native people has jumped an amazing 22% since 1996. We now account for 3.3% of the overall population of Canada, the second highest Indigenous percentage in the world next to the New Zealand Maori who account for a whopping 14% of their country. The most staggering of these statistics relates back to the Métis whose numbers have exploded by 43%. They now account for a third of all Canada's Aboriginals. That's 292,000 fiddle playing, spoon playing, jigging Métis, depending of course on how they are defined.

Analyzing the census, the National Post included a great quote by anthropologist Diamond Jenness who wrote in 1931, "Doubtless, all the tribes will disappear. Some will endure only a few years longer." Sounds like prohibition and that old belief that rock'n roll was just a fad.

I've heard it said that being born Native in this country is a political act in itself. I think it's important to add that being Native in this country is never boring. The Assembly of First Nations elections are coming up again. I'm already making popcorn.

WHO'S STEALING WHAT FROM WHO AND IS IT STEALING?

Cultural appropriation in the Arts has been a bugaboo in many a bonnet for the last fifteen years or so. The concept of somebody from one culture telling another culture's story has been discussed, argued, fought, and frequently dug up again to be rehashed in a dozen different ways. Often the major sticking point deals with when is enough enough. When does respect and political correction begin to infringe on the creative process so much in fact that it hampers, even compromises, the art? The argument often drifts to: should non-Native people write Native stories, should men write female characters, should heterosexuals write about the Gay experience, should dog people write about cat people? The lines of demarcation become blurrier than promises at closing time.

More recently, there's been a new development in the cultural appropriation issue; specifically, deep in the Native community. Renowned Cree playwright Tomson Highway is no stranger to the argument. He is a proponent of colour-blind casting and has often said art is colourless. This whole discussion annoys him to no end. In fact, several weeks ago at the Native Playwrights Summit in Toronto, he confessed that someday he plans to write a play in French with three white girls as the central characters.

This January, his first main stage play in fourteen years, titled *Ernestine Shuswap Gets Her Trout,* opens at the Western Theatre Company in Kamloops, British Columbia. The play takes place in Kamloops and all the major First Nations characters are Shuswap, Okanagan or Thompson. The playwright is Cree. Is this an issue? Somebody familiar with the area asked that question. Tomson said no. He had direct consultation with the local Aboriginal cultural centre to keep him honest.

Several months back, I was approached by the Toronto organization Red Sky Performance (a sister organization to Native Women in the Arts) which is run by the amazing Sandra Laronde. She asked if I would be interested in adapting the Tlingit creation story *How The Raven Stole The Sun* into a dance theatre piece for her company. I am Ojibway from the wilds of central Ontario and truth be told, I know very little about the Tlingit culture other than they are located along the northern B.C coast, as well as in Yukon and Alaska. I know there's probably salmon involved in the story.

Raven legends are ancient oral stories. The version I was to use was put down on paper by Alaskan Tlingit Maria Williams, who was flown into Toronto as a consultant for the original discussions. I asked Sandra if my being Ojibway (and herself, being from Temegami) would be an issue. Would we have hordes of politically correct Tlingit storming the Red Sky Performance offices? Sandra didn't think so. We were both Native, we were sensitive to the mistakes that could be made, and we had the blessing of Maria herself. But one Tlingit writer/actress/ storyteller that was at the Native Playwright's Summit said, "Why not get a Tlingit writer to do it? Hire me. What's their number?"

In my own and Tomson's defense, there is a sense of collective understanding that seems to exist between the First Nations of Canada regardless of what part of the country or Nation you are from. It's something akin to a sense of shared experiences, born of oppression, of survival, of disenfranchisement, of too much baloney. I believe this allows us to relate to each other's existence regardless of individual tribalism. We revel in our connection to this land.

My very first writing assignment, a thousand years ago, was for an episode of *The Beachcombers*. There I was, writing a story about Jesse Jim and his wife Laurel, two of the Native characters in the show. They were Salish if I remember correctly, I was not. I had never even been to British Columbia at that point. In the end, the episode turned out pretty good and I managed not to culturally embarrass myself.

I was also a writer on *North Of 60*, a show about the Dene of North West Territories. Again, I was not Dene, (unless there is something my Ojibway mother has not been telling me.) A Dene critic of the show was once quoted as saying "It's a show about my people written by Jews and Crees." And, I guess, unbeknownst to him, one lone Ojibway.

It seems that when you're writing a script for television, or some form of the dominant cultural media, the specifics of your Nation becomes irrelevant. Non-native producers seem only to care that you can wave around a status card and can tell the difference between a bagel and bannock. Ojibways can write about the Dene' or whoever.

The Haida can write about the Innu. I can even write about White people if I've got the inclination. Hey, I've been known to throw a few Caucasians into my scripts, just for lack of colour, and to find out if anybody would accuse me of culturally appropriating Burlington culture. Hasn't happened yet.

The ears prick up in our own community when we Native writers start looking over the fence at other First Nations stories. One woman on my Reserve was a little uncomfortable with the idea when I raised it, but then shook it off saying "Well, at least you, being the writer, will be Native. That's something." Maybe it is something. Maybe it's nothing. It is a question for those far more intelligent then I am. In the meantime, I've got an idea for a story about a handicapped Black Albino lesbian from South Africa... but it,s okay, her car has a dream-catcher hanging from the rearview mirror.

A WHALE OF A PROBLEM

When dynamite was invented by Alfred Nobel, he envisioned it as saving lives. It had been his intention to make mining and tunnel building far safer through the use of a more stable explosive. It grieved him enormously how his child had been turned into a weapon of death and destruction. Almost as penance, it was he, using the profits from that same invention, who set up the Nobel Peace Prize. The internet could be called the dynamite of the late twentieth and early twenty-first centuries. Once developed as a method of communication and information research, it has taken on many darker uses. The police regularly patrol cyberspace in search of child pornographers and hate groups amongst other questionable sites.

One such "hate" group now sharing its dubious opinions has, currently and in the past, issues with the Makah, an Aboriginal nation in Washington State. In 1999, this Native tribe reinstated their cultural practice of whale hunting, after a seventy-five-year hiatus. Many anti-whaling advocates actively and publicly disagreed with the Makah's decision to renew it's ancestral hunt. This battle spilled onto the internet where, for the price of a cup of air, anybody can voice an anonymous opinion. This includes a gentleman who goes by the online name ChristopherL. He rather eagerly insists on sharing some of his more unique perceptions of the Makah people, and all Indigenous people in general.

What follows are some of his more revealing arguments in his deceleration of superiority; in reference to some Native person wanting to start a band. "I shall call them `the indigenous whiners'... in order to have a band, somebody has to know about music. Music, scales, octaves, harmonies, tempo... Tone deaf grunting and random stomping won't satisfy the DJ's, and that's what the indigenous do." What this has to do with whaling, I'm not sure.

"You are not in a position to discuss culture, since yours (oh half-breed) does not exist. No music, no art, no literature, no dance, no technology, nothing except inflicting cruelty on anything you can catch. You grunt and sweat, leave your poop around to entertain anthropologist... abuse women, lie steal and since someone gave you a second-hand computer –spend your days lurking around children's sites, trying to lure a little girl to a playground somewhere."

"Rest assured that I do not want to be an Indian. Some human cultures are superior to others, and this is not racism – it is obvious fact. Your "culture" even lags behind the Euro and Asian cultures of 6,000 years ago. So long as you huddle in a group and refuse to try to better your lives, you will remain a sideshow exhibit of others... I do not want to be your friend because you are inferior. I imagine that everyone who has met you feels the same way. You sacrifice animals! ...I have rejected you totally as an inferior hominoid, somewhat like the Neanderthal, and destined for extinction."

"I am American. All members of my family are American. Our culture is American. We like our culture. We look down on yours. I do not look like you. I do not have short bow legs. I do not have flipper feet. I do not have missing fingers and toes. I do not have pockmarks. My head is not too large for my body. I am not fat. My hair is not greasy. I have a neck. I do not have tattoos. You are stupid. You kill animals to worship your god. You have no morals. Your language has no word for *wrong*." Print this out. Save it for your lawyer. Save it for your witch doctor. Save it for your parole officer. Or take it with you to your next pow wow with the dim hope that you might find some one who can read better than you. I have slipped into using big words and long sentences again. I can't even fake being as stupid as you."

"Examining human (more or less) fecal matter is how anthropologist discovered what Indians really ate –and it wasn't whale meat –or any other big game. You ate mice complete with bones –and every sort of intestinal parasites, along with snakes, insects, birds with feathers still on, grubs, dogs, and human flesh. Your feces were available, a thousand year's worth, because you never learned to bury it. Thank you for your contribution to science. It was the only one you made. I have added to your limited education and I hope you are chagrined enough to go to school. Always happy to help the underprivileged. And you truly are. By choice... there are reasons for your problems, but you will never see them. You would have to stop giving birth to FAS first."

"Indians rob, rape, and kill each other at greater rates than you want anyone to know. Who else would bother? What have you got that anyone wants to take? Who goes to your reservations for any reason at all. The prisons are full of Indians...and the numbers would be even greater if the reservation police made any attempt to preserve law and order. But since they are often convicted felons themselves, what could one expect?"

"What's the problem?

"O GREAT CREATOR SEND A WHALE, BUT HECK I THINK WHILE I'M WAITING I'LL PICK UP MY WELFARE CHECK!" This is funny. Some people are superior to others, and that's that."

Others have entered the discussion adding their own little pearls of wisdom. Alfred Dunn offers "And since the North American Indians did not work metal, they could not have gardening tools, so they had to rely on what they found lying around in open spaces... they used pointed sticks to dig up tubers. But you didn't learn. You didn't farm. What a crock. You had no tools, no means of clearing land, and the men were too lazy. THEY PICKED STUFF UP OFF THE GROUND LIKE EVERY OTHER STONE AGE GROUP. They are Stone Age people. Look at them. It astounds me that any of them have even learned to drive. The tires must be constant sources of magic in their eyes. "Things go round and round and I go in ditch. Damn Whitey! He can't build anything right."

"You don't like it... MOVE. Go back to your reservation, build a wall around you, give back the jeans you are wearing, the automobile you drive and slip on something comfortable like a loin cloth...This is AMERICA and we are all AMERICANS if you want to be Indian then do so but stop bitching at us because you can't make it on your own". And SimonW2001 defends the argument with the astute observation that "of course, you did not eat whales! Unless, and of course, they died and washed up. You did not have gunboats and fifty-caliber guns at the time. So you were not able to kill them. You ate mice and so you should continue to do so. Only say that you wish to continue your ancestral diet and we shall be of aid to you."

Does this make me angry? No, I actually find it funny. It's amazing what a little... very little knowledge can do. The Mayans never forged metal, but they invented the "zero" centuries before anybody else, and had a calender that up until fairly recently was the most precise in the world. When they weren't digging up tubers with pointed sticks of course.

Should you wish to register your opinion or investigate, just go to http.//certain-natl.org/morequotes.html, if it's still around, Neanderthals need not apply.

THE THINGS YOU LEARN WHEN NOT IN SCHOOL

"Education is an admirable thing, but it is well to remember from time to time that nothing worth knowing can be taught."
Oscar Wilde

One day while I was having lunch at the Governor General's Rideau Hall Residence (it's not often I get to start a story like this), I bumped into Matthew Coon Come, Grand Chief of the Assembly of First Nations at the time. While we chatted, he mentioned hearing my name and asked what I did for a living. I summed up a fifteen year writing career into a few sentences about being a playwright with a dozen books and over fifty productions of plays to my credit. He seemed mildly impressed and then asked where I'd gone to University. That's when the bubble burst.

I told him I never went to University, that I was a member of the great uneducated masses. Everything I learned, I had learned by being a student of life. The tuition was cheaper. He laughed and said something like: well, there goes that idea. I asked, "What idea?" He said that for a moment he thought I might be a great role model for Aboriginal youth. Evidently the idea quickly evaporated due to a noticeable lack of degrees.

This reminded me of a similar incident several years earlier which occurred at a birthday party for a professor at York University. The slightly tipsy birthday boy, an expert on Native literature, asked how I could validate myself as a contemporary playwright whose work was being studied in many different universities without having any academic credentials behind my name. It seemed he thought the situation was an ironic oxymoron. I didn't take his comments personally, since the alcohol and potato chips were free.

It is a touchy subject for many people. The definition of what proper education consists of. There is a universally accepted belief that education is important in many cultures in societies. Especially in today's society when technology, politics, economics and practically everything changes on a yearly basis. Education is good. The more the merrier. Especially in the Native community which suffers an appalling school drop out rate. What often puzzles me is the narrow definition of what is considered acceptable education.

At one time amongst Aboriginal people, education often came from the Elders. Everything we were taught came directly from those who had experienced it. Many still follow that tradition and understand the importance of using diverse sources of knowledge. For example, Matthew Coon Come's homecoming to his people, the James Bay Cree, is now part of Aboriginal folklore. Returning home from McGill and Trent University where he studied Law, Political Science, Economics and Native Studies, Matthew's father promptly took him out onto the land to complete an equally important part of his education. Unfortunately, not everyone understands the variety of educational opportunities out there and potential venues of education are ignored in favour of popular European models.

In the Ontario Aboriginal community of Curve Lake, a prime example of this contradiction is running it's course. A young woman named Pattie Shaughnessy applied to the Band's Education Committee for funding to attend the Centre for Indigenous Theatre's (CIT) Native Theatre School, an organization devoted to teaching young Native people the art of theatre from both contemporary and Native perspectives. To be fair, I must admit a conflict of issues here. I am a member of the Curve Lake First Nations with several relatives on the Education committee; I am also on the Board of Directors for the CIT. I should also point out that I know Ms. Shaughnessy casually.

Ms. Shaughnessy, an aspiring actress with solid ambitions, was turned down by the committee. She has also recently auditioned for the prestigious National Theatre School in Montreal, and I thought supporting such a lady in her artistic endeavors would be a real feather in the community's cap. Evidently I was wrong. As a board member, who had written Ms Shaugnessy a letter of support, I pursued the issue in an informal manner and was told the education committee prefers to financially support applications only to accredited institutions. This committee policy was told it was a way to make sure students and the Band didn't throw their money away on "fly-by-night organizations." I informed the woman I was talking to that the Native Theatre School had been around since 1974 and practically every Aboriginal actor in Canada had once been a student there. "Then get the place accredited," was the response. When Ms. Shaughnessy informed them that a good chunk of CIT's funding came from federal, rather than provincial, sources which limited eligibility for accreditation. "Then tell them to get provincial funding." Ahh. If only the world were so cut and dried. During a discussion later with a senior committee member, I asked how many of the Education Committee members had any post-secondary school education, to which I received what seemed to be an oddly indignant but firm, "that's completely irrelevant." Irrelevant." As an artist, I liken it to someone with reasonable arts experience or background, sitting on an arts adjudication panel. You would think it would just make sense to know of which you judge.

Luckily this is not a policy held by too many Native communities. In the past, Rama First Nation in Ontario has funded students to the CIT. For the last two years, Wahpeton Dakota Nation in Central Saskatchewan has not only funded at least five students a year, but has also hosted CIT's summer theatre school. They understand not all forms of education have lecture halls and tests or involve tossing a graduation cap into the air.

In the end, it's not a matter of which form of education is better or worse. I'm sure Grand Chief Coon Come appreciates that both forms of learning are equally valuable. It's a pity more people don't.

"Training is everything. The peach was once a bitter almond; cauliflower is nothing but cabbage with a college education."
Mark Twain

WHEN THE LAUGHTER STOPS

Some people have no sense of humour. Just ask Bernie Francis. He's the Mi'kmaq gentleman who last year caused a bit of a fuss at the annual Treaty Days Festival in the Maritimes. Being somewhat of a grassroots social critic, Francis rewrote and sang a version of Sinatra's "I Did It My Way" which lampooned the huge salaries and expense accounts of two local Chiefs; money that allegedly exceeded $400,000. He called his version of the song "I Hid It My Way."

It is said that truth is beauty and beauty is truth. Well, not for Bernie. For being such a bad and truthful boy he was sent to the proverbial corner and forbidden to play. In other words, he was barred from performing at the festival this year. And to add insult to injury, all First Nation performers were forced to sign a contract which forbid them from cracking jokes or satirizing Aboriginal leaders during the Sept. 30th Festival. Performers were warned that anyone who breaks the prohibition wouldn't be paid their concert fee. Hmmm. Me thinks somebody is a little sensitive. To paraphrase the immortal words of my fellow playwright William Shakespeare, Me think they doth protest too much.

As a humorist and satirist, this particular issue strikes close to home and inflames my sense of injustice. I don't know how to get rid of the inflammation. Granted there is a time and place for humour as well as for respect. Humour is to amuse not abuse. However, a musical festival does not strike me as a particularly solemn or serious event where social humour should be prohibited. For those of an older generation, Woodstock, with it's various musical/political protests, comes to mind. I understand Treaty Days is not Woodstock. Less nudity and mud, but the principle of freedom of expression is still the same.

According to reports, Bernie Francis's song brought the house down. The audience loved it. Maybe two or three people didn't, for obvious reasons. Therefore, they changed the rules to suit their needs. Shame, shame. If I remember my Star Trek pop references, "the needs of the many outweigh the needs of the few." Gee, a singer who is creative, talented and loved by the audience. No wonder he was banned! I'm surprised he got away so lightly. What these people no doubt forgot is the long tradition which mockery and teasing have in Native cultures.

The various Trickster representations common to so many of our Nations comes to mind. Those who have visited the pueblos of the American Southwest will tell you of a sacred clown figure called a koshare, a very important figure in Pueblo cosmology. Select members of the village dress in horizontally striped black and white outfits and make-up for certain ceremonies. These characters comically entertain the audience by showing how people tend to do everything wrong and that only the spirits are perfect. One of their duties is to illustrate the dangers of greed, and materialism. Their symbolic function is to keep the community honest by pointing out foibles and greed. Part of their function is to humble those who need to be, thus maintaining the harmony of the community. Darn clever, them Pueblo people.

I don't know if Bernie Francis cares about koshares or even Shakespeare, but what may be of interest to him are the words an Elder from Alberta's Blood Reserve who said "Humour is the WD-40 of healing." I guess with a salary of $400,000, they can afford to get a better doctor or to buy the whole hospital.

MY ELDER IS BETTER THAN YOUR ELDER

It seems that in the simple world of Eldership (i.e. the fine art of being an Aboriginal Elder), there is a hierarchy that I was not aware of. This hierarchy recently became apparent when I was involved in a conversation about a certain Elder who shall remain nameless for obvious reasons. This one individual openly scoffed at the idea of this person being considered a wise and respected Elder citing the fact that he was a raging alcoholic once. "He was the worst drunk in the village!"

Now it's no surprise to anyone how one's past experiences and mistakes can follow you for the rest of your life. Elders are no different. Mistakes are buoys on the river of life that can help you either navigate the river or send you up shit creek without a paddle.

I didn't realize how those mistakes can also negate the positive achievements a person might accomplish during the remaining days of their existence. I was truly surprised to find that only those who never drank, never lied, never abused tobacco, never swore, never walked counter-clockwise at a clockwise ceremony or were ever human could be considered the only real Elders. I learn something new everyday.

I suppose priests and nuns who hear their calling late in life can't really become true priests and nuns since, more than likely, at some time in their past they've either taken the Lord's name in vain, had sex with a Protestant or sampled some Devil's Food cake... maybe all three at once.

It is no secret the best drug and alcohol counselors are people who have lived the darker side of life and know of what they speak. Otherwise, counselling sessions would be like learning to water-ski by someone afraid of the water. You can read all you want and take as many workshops as you like but unless you've wrestled with those demons yourself, there's only so much hands-on experience you can bring to the job. Which is why I'm puzzled by this reaction to an Elder who had a life before they became an Elder.

Handsome Lake, a Seneca Chief in the late 1700's considered by many Iroquois to be the second great messenger after the Peacemaker himself, was sent to his people by the Creator to teach the wisdom of the Great Peace, part of the Iroquois philosophy/beliefs. Yet, his vision came to him during a four-day coma induced by a rather severe bout of drinking. The point being Handsome Lake cleaned up his act to become a well respected orator and teacher. Gandhi, a different type of Indian I'm fairly certain can be included in the classification of wise Elder, was a lawyer before he became the man of peace we are all familiar with. Now that's a hell of a bigger obstacle to overcome than alcoholism. Buddha was a spoiled prince before he saw the light, walked the path of wisdom and developed a big belly.

Perhaps it was Nietzsche, (who may or may not be considered an elder, depending on your philosophical learnings) who said it best when he wrote the rather over used cliché, "that which does not destroy us, makes us stronger." Maybe Nietzsche was an elder because that certainly sounds like many an elder's story I've heard. The fortitude I find in many elders can only be forged from experience and suffering.

I believe it was William Blake who coined the term, "The palace of wisdom lies on the road of excess." Wisdom comes from experience. Experience comes through trial and error. Sometimes error means waking up in a place you don't know, smelling like something you don't want to and realizing you might not have many more mornings left to wake up to. You have to travel before you know the countryside.

Several years ago I attended an Elder's conference where a bunch of us in a large room waited to be instilled with knowledge by a visiting Elder whose name I have forgotten. Several young people took out pen and paper, ready to diligently learn. This method of learning was not to be. The Elder quietly asked them to put their note pads away. "Writing something down is asking permission to forget it", he said. It made sense. A few days ago, I came across a quote in a newspaper. I think the quote was from Plato, that ancient Greek philosopher dude from twenty-five hundred years ago, who said, "Writing is the instrument of forgetfulness." Sound familiar? –Two wise individuals from primarily oral cultures. It seems great minds do think alike.

What is an Elder? How do you define one? Some say you can't be one until you are a grandfather, while other's say it has to be conferred upon you by the community, not by self-identification. I've heard it

said there's an inner glow that you recognize. Perhaps a more important question is, "Who has the authority to say somebody isn't an
Elder?" Let ye who is without wisdom, cast the first doubt.

GETTING TO THE *ART* OF THE MATTER
(VISITING YOUR ARTISTIC NATURE PERSERVE)

WHEN WAS THE LAST TIME YOU SAW A NAKED INDIAN

Naked Native people; you don't see a lot of them. I'm talking about their representation in television, theatre or print. Even more so, it's Native men who are remarkably absent from baring all to the world. Some time back when I was writing a play titled *alterNATIVES*, my girlfriend at the time was complaining how the media was always flaunting naked or near naked women at every possible chance, but seldom men. And when they did, it was seldom that anything remotely interesting of the man was ever shown but was only hinted at. Unlike women where you couldn't throw a rock without hitting a boob or a feminine behind. It wasn't that my girlfriend wanted to see a lot of naked men, it was more about the disproportional delineation of nudity. It was a political statement, she said... yeah, right.

Respectful of her concerns, I attempted to do my little bit to rectify that little issue in my own little way. My play *alterNATIVES* now begins with a good looking naked young Native man cartwheeling onto the stage from the bedroom.

"Now how's that for an entrance," I thought. Unfortunately, my feminist-supportive intentions were thwarted from an unexpected source –the actors. In the two productions of that play to date, the two lead actors, good looking young men with nothing to be embarrassed about, refused to do the scripted entrance. Instead, they did the cartwheel in their underwear. Both said the play was supposed to be a drama, not a comedy.

I began to think that maybe there was a logical reason for the limited amount of male Aboriginal skin out there. A year or two later, a play was produced in Toronto that called for all six of its actors (three male, three female) to be naked. I had fond recollections of a ground-breaking play from the 1970s that was one of the first in Canada to feature naked people on stage (White people though). This time around, one of the cast members was a Native man. Several weeks into the rehearsal he confessed to the director and the rest of the cast that he couldn't do the nude scenes and offered to pull out of the show. With some encouragement and creative blocking from the cast and director, he stayed in the show while maintaining his modesty. The odd thing about the show was that everyone else at various times, whether separately or together, were exceedingly naked except (noticeably) him. This made him stand out even more... so to speak.

Are Native men more shy than Native women? The only possible contradiction I can think of is Gary Farmer, Cayuga actor and media mogul. An exception to the rule perhaps. This man has appeared naked on stage and screen more times than I have at home. Anyone who's seen *Pow Wow Highway* or *Dead Man* are familiar with his cinematic backside. Add to that the various productions of Tomson Highway's play *Drylips Oughta Move to Kapuskasing* where he appears on stage wearing nothing but a frying pan. At the beginning of the play when the lights come up, this is the first image you see of the play and of Mr. Farmer. For good or bad, I'm sure it was many Caucasian theatre patron's introduction to Native theatre.

The reason this has been on my mind recently is because of a documentary I've been researching for the National Film Board of Canada. The focus is Native erotica; more specifically, the reclaiming of Native sexuality. One of the avenues I want to explore deals with storytelling since many traditional stories were bawdy and unabashedly sexual in nature. I want to juxtapose this with the way Native people are manifesting their contemporary sexuality today. Someone suggested was a photo shoot might capture these elements.

I found a Native photographer who had always wanted to shoot a nude photography session for artistic reasons. He made me a deal. He was a happily married, middle-aged man with a young daughter and didn't feel comfortable going up to beautiful Native women and ask them to pose naked. He wanted me to do it. "Fine," I said, "I'll be the dirty old man." I was nervous about being in this position too but felt it was integral to making a point in the documentary. That being said, it was the easiest thing I have ever done. I casually mentioned my dilemma to a few people and since then, without even trying to locate models, I have received three or four offers from women interested in participating. One reputable and intelligent volunteer said "And I'm sure my younger sister would be interested too."

In the play *Drylips Oughta Move to Kapuskasing*, there is a table dance/striptease performed by a woman in the cast. In the movie *Dead Man*, a lovely woman flashes her behind. There are or were two Native porn actresses working in the States. What does this mean in the larger picture? That most Native male actors and performers are afraid to take their clothes off on stage... except Gary Farmer? That Native women have no problem with nudity? To tell you the truth, I wouldn't do the cartwheel in my own play, but then again, I just don't want to embarrass all the other men.

ON WHY I WRITE

I never thought I'd be a writer. Both my mother and grade ten English teacher told me there wasn't much future in it for me, so I put that dream on the back burner for almost a decade. In the meantime, I read. I always read. I couldn't imagine not reading. Growing up on a Reserve in Central Ontario, Canada, there was little else to do. When I was five years old, my mother would bring me home comic books. Lots and lots of comic books. I sat on the steps in the living room looking at the bright exciting images on the pages trying to figure out what the story was. I was so excited because the next year I would be going to school. It wouldn't be long before I would be able to actually read the comic books, not just study the dramatic drawings. *It's interesting the memories that stick with you.*

Aggressive reading wasn't a big pastime on my Reserve. I read so much my grandparents told my mother that she shouldn't let me read so much. "It's not normal," they said. I read everything. I was the only kid in my school who had read all twenty-four *Tarzan of the Apes* novels, all twelve of the *Conan the Barbarian* series, the original *Frankenstein* and a host of other novels of questionable virtue. Not exactly fodder for an award winning Aboriginal playwright, but inspiration can be found in the most unexpected places. I'm a firm believer that storytelling is storytelling, whether is Hemingway or Lovecraft. In the end, it's just a matter of taking the audience on a journey of words... and I've always loved to travel.

Chances are, I'll never make it to the African jungle, especially one mysteriously absent of bugs and where a single White man rules the land omnipotently. Quite conceivably, I'll also never bullfight in Spain or engage in an epic sword fight except through the power of the written word. Why else would you read, except for the adventure!

Believe it or not, this is coming from a person who was raised in an oral culture where the storyteller (or orator) was king and the written word a mere pretender to the throne. At an Elder's conference I attended, an Elder began to lecture when he noticed a young woman starting to take notes. The Elder gently urged her to put her pen away,

"Writing something down is asking permission to forget it" he said, which basically invalidated my whole career.

As a writer I'm often asked where I went to University, or what my degree is in. I have neither been to University or have a degree, because I consider each book on my shelf a degree.

Theatrical Postcards From America

It's no secret that the three largest human exports to the United States are hockey players, comedians and Native playwrights (or, by proxy, their Native plays). Almost unheard of in the States, researchers and a few hardy theatre eccentrics had to look northward to get an Aboriginal theatre fix. Which is the reason why I found myself on a cold New England evening making my way through the narrow streets of Providence, Rhode Island to see a public reading of *The Buz'gem Blues*, an Aboriginal comedy I wrote.

On January 24th, Trinity Repertory Theatre, one of the five largest repertory theatres in America with an annual budget of 7.6 million, hosted its second annual Theatre From The Four Directions Festival. Last year's festival included Assiniboine/Nakota playwright William Yellow Robe Jr., the company's Playwright-In-Residence, and two Canadian Native writers, Saulteaux playwright and winner of the 1997 Governor General's Award, Ian Ross (who for some reason neglected to show up) and myself. Representatives from theatres and educational institutions in America's northeast came to the sold-out festival to check out this strange animal called Native theatre. Now, based on the success of both festivals, a full scale production of one of these plays is planned for next season with a possible national tour to follow. If so, this will be the largest production of a Native play in the States. Cherokee director and Yale School of Drama graduate Elizabeth Theobald Richards says it will definitely be one for the record books.

Although relatively rare, Aboriginal involvement in theatre is not entirely unknown down south. American Indian writers Diane Glancy, William Yellow Robe Jr. and Hanay Geiogama have been plying their artistic wares for years, with limited results, in an environment unaware there were Native people living in the States, let alone ones who had anything interesting to portray on stage.

Randy Reinholz, Artistic Director and co-founder with Jean Bruce Scott of Native Voices, an American Indian theatre company and Festival located in San Diego and Los Angeles, believes, "Native Theatre in the States is like Native people in the States, we're struggling to even have anybody notice we are not extinct. While we were doing Maria Clement's (Canadian playwright) show Urban Tattoo at the Gene Autry Heritage Museum in L.A., the museum did a market survey of what were the common perceptions about Native Americans in Los Angeles and Southern California. And the most common perception is that they didn't know there were Native people. They thought they were extinct. So when you think that's what popular Americans think, the idea of Native theatre is really way out there. It's kind of an esoteric thing."

Oskar Eustis, Artistic director of Rhode Island's Trinity Repertory Theatre has a similar spin on the theory. "...in the United States, there is a much lower level of sophistication about culture, about the idea that the government should be involved within an ongoing investment and supportive of. So it makes it tougher on any group that doesn't have financial resources or critical masses to find a voice in entering the mainstream. As a result, I feel like we haven't gotten a movement here yet.... I look at Tomson Highway's breakthrough plays in the mid-1980s and it's an event that seemed to catalyze Canadian Native theatre. We haven't had that founding bomb go off."

The bomb may be ticking. These days, the Native theatrical voice seems to appear disproportionately more often south of the border, but it's a Canadian Native voice. Reinholz's Native Voices, in operation since 1993, has workshopped and presented twenty-four scripts in total with about half by Canadian Native playwrights. The company is in preproduction for a third Equity production in L.A., with two of those three productions featuring Canadian writers.

Oddly enough, the presence of Canadian Native writers in American theatre system is not going unnoticed. Reinholz's Board of Directors have been heard to complain about the high percentage of Canadians the American organization seems to support. During the late 1990s I was invited twice to participate in the Prince William Sound Community College Edward Albee Theatre Conference held in Valdez, Alaska. I was there both times to accept first prize in the Alaska Native Plays Contest. During my last visit, one of the organizers told me the rules for the competition were going to be changed. A member of the University of Alaska faculty who organized the conference commented with some irritation, if they were going to become a dumping ground for Canadian Indian playwrights? I have not been back since.

Canadian Native writers have a greater history, a longer history of combining storytelling with contemporary theatre. The scripts are easier to work with because the writers have a long history of working in theatre. When we work with a lot of the writers from the States, I would say with half of them it's their first or second workshop. So there was a kind of getting everybody on the same page process of 'what do you do to workshop.' "And the Canadians had already been through this process, very familiar with the process and very able to use it properly," commented Reinholz. "Additionally, the writers have been known for a while. Canadian writers have been published and people have been writing about Canadian Native theatre for ten years. It's part of the mainstream. There's also a deeper talent pool, both acting and I think there's an emerging directing, and I bet there'll be a designing pool and stage managers, so there's quite an interesting pool to draw from in Canada."

The result of the Canadian First Nations theatrical influx into the American theatrical heart... who knows? We might end up being just a momentary blip on the scope or we might actually develop into a legitimate trend. It's too early to say. Time will tell.

In a further search for Native theatre in America, after Rhode Island I saddled up my pony and forayed over to the next logical destination in my theatrical sojourn... New York City's Broadway. You won't find more theatres and plays per capita than the theatre district around Times Square. As expected, there was nary a Native play to be seen. Perhaps that's why it's called the Great White Way.

The journey was not without discovery. I found out that New York's Smithsonian Museum of the American Indian plans to further explore the possibility of utilizing more Native theatre into their mandate.

On an ironic note, the museum is located on the edge of Wall Street, a street which got its name several hundred years ago because originally there was a large wall built on that location to keep the Indians out. Even more ironic while at the Smithsonian Museum of the American Indian I bumped into, of all people, the Honourable Robert Nault, the Canadian Federal Minister of Indian and Northern Development. DIAND's just got to know what all the Indian are up to, regardless of where they are.

SCENT OF AN INDIAN

Advertising is often described as a barometer of what is on our minds. It's a window into pop culture. Television and radio commercials, magazine ads and bus shelter posters tell us a lot about what people want and what they are buying. Which is why I am perplexed about a new billboard I've seen scattered throughout the city of Toronto. That seems to defeat the purpose of advertising as well as culturally misappropriating a ubiquitous Aboriginal symbol.

Several weeks ago I noticed a huge billboard high above Church Street, just south of Wellesley promoting a new type of perfume by the Lise Watier company called "Capteur de Reve". Translated into English the product is named Dreamcatcher. On that same billboard, to illustrate the kind of individual who evidently wears this perfume, was what appeared to me to be the image of a young, bone-thin woman (whom I assume was supposed to be First Nations) squatting on her heels, looking into space with disinterest and what seemed to be feathers tucked into her braided hair. She was wearing a loin cloth. Worst of all, the film used to photograph her was brown, and heavily textured which gave the impression she was very dirty. No doubt, this model represented the target audience to which they were aiming. Speaking as an Aboriginal male, this image produced the opposite effect of what the perfume was no doubt attempting to generate. I found nothing alluring in the ad to make me think, "Boy, now there's a woman I would love to smell." Perhaps if I drank the perfume first. A lot of it.

On a political level I do not object to the use of Native imagery or models to sell products, as long as it is done tastefully. I know too many unemployed actors and models to say what they can and can't do. God knows the dreamcatcher entered the public domain years ago. You no longer have to be Native to have one dangling from your rear view mirror –although it helps. The dreamcatcher's original purpose was to be hung above the bed of a newly married couple or a new born baby. This allowed good dreams to pass through the web and bad dreams to be caught and dissolved by the morning light. A charming and entertaining story, but there is no mention of a squatting woman in it.

Maybe it's me but to tell you the truth, the image of a dirty woman with quail feathers sticking out of her hair (I have to mention it again) *squatting* on the ground does little to entice me. This is not the dream I want my dreamcatcher to catch. I think the idea of a perfume called Capteur de Reve/Dreamcatcher is a fine idea, but surely they could have come up with far better visual imagery. I know beauty and attraction is truly in the eye of the beholder... but did I mention she was *squatting*? The word and the image is not that conducive to intimacy. Also she was far too thin to be taken seriously in the Native community where the Gwyneth Paltrow/Calista Flockhart school of thought does not hold sway and the women do not believe calories are only for the poor, but are aware of the benefits of soup and water.

On a more puzzling note, a Native woman I know commented when she saw the billboard "Is that supposed to be a woman?" There is an unmistakable androgynous quality to the figure; enough of one that another female friend of mine declared, "That's a man. Look at the hair on the arms, the shoulders and collar bone. That's gotta be a man." Beside the squatting figure (with knees hiding the chest area) reads, quite plainly, "For Women." However, the poster is in the Church/Wellesley area of Toronto (an area highly populated by the gay community) so anything might be up for grabs.

Now putting the sexual shoe on the other foot, will Capteur de Reve/Dreamcatcher perfume attract many semi-naked androgynous dirty men with feathers in their hair who like to squat. Maybe Lise Watier needs to consider a new marketing campaign. Of course, this could be one of those ambidextrous/unisex kind of perfumes that doesn't see the need for X or Y chromosome limitations. After all, in the dark, we all smell alike. Perhaps the best description of this poster came from another friend of mine who said, somewhat graphically, "It looks like she's taking a dump." Just thirty more days of shopping left until Christmas. Look for Capteur de Reve/Dreamcatcher at your finer perfume salons.

THE "MOST INFLUENTIAL AND ESSENTIAL" LIST:
EVERYTHING YOU NEED TO KNOW IN THE NATIVE ARTS
COMMUNITY

The success of *Atanarjuat: The Fast Runner*, at the Cannes Film Festival proved something very interesting –the Native voice is running rampant in this country (and abroad) and is taking no prisoners. Around the same time, Ian Ross received the Governor General's Award for Best Play for *fareWell*, as well the critical popularity of *Green Grass Running Water* by Thomas King is all proof that Native artists have left the Reserve and are launching a land claim smack dab in the middle of Canada's artistic community. So many new expressions of Aboriginal creativity are currently available to the public that, it's easy to get lost in the shopping aisles of the First Nations artistic supermarket. Fear no more, for I will provide some home delivery.

Below are a series of lists put together by Aboriginal experts in their field. The suggestions from these experts are what they consider *essential* material for those interested in aboriginal arts. This compilation is not meant to be *the* definitive list, nor the final one, but merely educated suggestions involving a veritable cornucopia of genres and artists. Consider them a primer for those who want to be in the loop and spice up their dinner party conversation.

THE TOP 5 ESSENTIAL ABORIGINAL DOCUMENTARIES
COMPLIED BY CYNTHIA LICKERS

Cynthia Lickers is a Turtle clan woman from Six Nations Reserve. She is the former Artistic Director of the Centre for Aboriginal Media and the imagineNATIVE Media Arts Festival.

Kanehsatake: 270 Years of Resistance **by Alanis Obomsawin**
In 1990, the Mohawk people of Kanehsatake held ground against the Canadian Army over the town of Oka's proposed expansion of a golf course on a sacred burial ground. This film documented an event which captured the world's attention. It won numerous awards and was instrumental in providing a path for Aboriginal people who wanted to have their stories heard from the first person's point of view.

98

***Richard Cardinal: Cry from a Diary of a Métis Child* by Alanis Obomsawin**
This film shares the lost feelings one child has while being placed in foster homes until he eventually commits suicide. This film changed the adoption policy.

***Donna's Story* by Doug Cuthand**
A former prostitute, and drug addict changes her life and sets out to change the fate of others. This film has helped get Aboriginal people off the streets.

***Forgotten Warriors* by Loretta Todd**
Forgotten Warriors shares the injustices endured by Aboriginal soldiers returning from World War II. This film is a *real* war story.

***The Return of Navajo Boy* by Bennie Klain**
This touching story is about a home movie lost for many years and one man's search to find the people filmed. A family reunites after someone reads their story in a newspaper. This film is a look into the meaning of family to an Aboriginal person.

THE TOP 5 ESSENTIAL NATIVE PLAYS
COMPLIED BY KENNETCH CHARLETTE

Kennetch Charlette, an actor, playwright and director is currently the Artistic Director of Saskatchewan Native Theatre Company in Saskatoon.

***The Rez Sisters* by Tomson Highway**
I believe *The Rez Sisters* was written to honour the women of Native ancestry. The play made an impact on me in such a way that I could relate the characters and storyline to my own family and community. It reiterated that the dysfunctions of my family and people in my community had to change their ways. This play was a turning point for my own personal growth.

Dry Lips Oughta Move To Kapuskasing by **Tomson Highway**

Dry Lips is one I chose for probably the same reasons most people did... either they hated it or loved it due to the controversy. The reality of life on the Rez was either too much to handle for most people or too humorous to be real. The symbolism of the oppression and rape of a people is forever etched in my mind.

Only Drunks and Children Tell The Truth by **Drew Hayden Taylor**

Only Drunks was a play written about the scoop up of Native children. This is an issue that I can relate to in my personal life as many of my relatives were victims of this tragedy. The humour and wit by which the play was written balanced the positive and negative aspects. Truly enjoyable and one of the best plays Drew has ever written.

fareWell by **Ian Ross**

fareWell is a play written by an aspiring playwright who was a newcomer to the theatre scene. Ian Ross displayed a style of writing that rivaled the established writers of the day which made him a force to be reckoned with. The play is bold, touching, revealing and honest. These qualities reveal a great playwright willing to take risks in bringing truth to life.

The Ecstasy of Rita Joe by **George Ryga**

The Ecstasy of Rita Joe was the first play I read about Native people. This story allowed me to believe that Native people did have a voice beyond "How". An inspiration to me.

THE TOP 5 ESSENTIAL ABORIGINAL MOVIES
BY DARREL DENNIS

Darrel Dennis is a Shuswap writer, actor, comedian and host of the popular APTN series "Bingo and a Movie."

Once Were Warriors

A Maori woman struggles to hold her family together in the face of domestic violence, sexual abuse, gangs and the Maori class systems. Although not technically a native American movie, it is almost an identical representation of the struggles facing the urban Native population. A brutally honest depiction of the results of urbanization and colonization. A must see for anyone ready to delve beyond the Hollywood mystification of this planet's First peoples.

The Doe Boy

A mixed-blood hemophiliac boy is faced with his own mortality when he learns that his blood infusions may have been tainted with HIV. A Sundance movie, very hard to acquire, but one of the most human and intelligent movies about Native people ever made. Not only does this movie credit native people with intelligence but it also paints a very sympathetic picture of the Native lead's white father. Very refreshing to see a realistic and loving relationship between a Native and white character based on human emotion instead of issues. The acting and writing is superb and the cast is jaw-droppingly beautiful.

Atanarjuat: The Fast Runner

A tale of bad medicine and betrayal that takes place in the pre-contact Inuit north. If you like epic movies that last three hours then you'll love Atanarjuat. Filmed entirely on digital video, this movie follows the lives of three brothers and their feud with another family that results in murder, witchcraft, and coveting. Filmed entirely in the Inuit language and using all Inuit actors, this is an epic tale that would make Shakespeare proud.

Thunderheart

A native American F.B.I. agent is sent to the reservation to solve the murder of an Indian activist. Although it is never stated outright, the events and characters depicted in this movie are based on actual people and events from Wounded Knee and the Pine Ridge Reservation in South Dakota. If it were not for Val Kilmer's Cherokee heritage, this could have easily been another "White man saves the Indian" movie. Instead, the real story is about how the Indians open the eyes of the F.B.I. agent to governmental corruption. Well-written script, great action sequences, and a movie stealing performance by Graham Greene.

Dance Me Outside/Smoke Signals –aka: The Adam Beach snack pack. Two award winning contemporary films about native youth that highlight Adam Beach's best performances to date.:

Dance Me Outside

The lives of four Native teens are changed forever when the town racist murders their friend. Dance Me Outside is loosely based on the book by W.P. Kinsella. Although structurally flawed in the sense that the movie appears to screen as a series of short stories, the writing and cast more than make up for it. This is one of the first movies that young Native people were allowed to be sexy, and human. The characters are articulate, intelligent, and actually experience a range of emotions beyond stoic or criminal. Dance Me Outside proves that an entire film can rest on the shoulders of a Native cast without help from a non-Native "saviour".

Smoke Signals

Two young Native men travel across the country to attain closure after the death of one of the young men's father. The darling of the festival films, Smoke Signals has a tendency to sit in its own preciousness at times, but effectively presents the issue of absentee fathers in the Native community. Very entertaining movie, worthy of recognition for being one of the first ever studio films written by, directed by and starring natives.

THE FIVE ESSENTIAL ABORIGINAL POETS
BY DANIEL DAVID MOSES

Poet, playwright, editor and Delaware, Daniel David Moses calls both Toronto, Ontario, Canada and the Six Nations of the Grand River his home. His most recent poetry publication is *Sixteen Jesuses* (Exile Editions 2000.)

E. Pauline Johnson, the Mohawk who also had the temerity to be a Victorian Poetess, is still the earth in which First Nations poetry in Canada's English has its roots. Recommended *–Flint and Feather.*

Louise Halfe, who's been known to put on her accent to call the Pope `da Poop' but mostly speaks lyrically about the powers of Cree medicine and life's mysteries, is the rich soil in Saskatchewan where the poetry grows both sweet and tart. Recommended –*Bear Bones and Feathers.*

Greg Scofield, who mixes things up in English and Cree, a real metis-sage of contemporary street and old wisdom, is Rockies mineral-rich ground where the poetry grows fast, political, familiar, and oh so sexy. Recommended –*Love Medicine and One Song.*

Lenore Keeshig-Tobias, the Anishnabekwe who has the temerity to also be a story-teller, is that rock on which First Nations poetry dream-stories have persisted and insisted themselves, lovely and ageless as green moss. Recommended –*Native Poetry in Canada* (a sizable selection from Keeshig-Tobias and others listed as well.)

Michael Paul-Martin, who sings the vigor of the Oji-Cree Ontario wilderness into the over-tilled lawns of the city, is a land that's care-filled and sharp and secretly sunny. Recommended –*She Said, 'Sometimes I Hear Things'.*

THE FIVE ESSENTIAL ABORIGINAL NOVELS
BY KATERI AKIWENZIE-DAMM

Kateri Akiwenzie-Damm is a writer, publisher, and founder of the Honouring Words: International Indigenous Writers Celebration Tour which has been held in Canada in 2002 and Australia in 2003. The next international Honouring Words tour will be held in New Zealand in 2005. Kateri is from the Chippewas of Nawash First Nation.

In Search of April Raintree by Beatrice Culleton.
A classic in Aboriginal literature in Canada. Along with Maria Campbell's autobiographical *Halfbreed*, this is a must read for anyone with an interest in Aboriginal literature. Culleton and Campbell's books have influenced generations of Aboriginal writers and have left an indelible mark on the literary landscape in this country.

***Keeper n' Me* by Richard Wagamese.**
An entertaining first novel about a man going back to the Rez and proving you can't go home again –or can you? Flawed, as most first novels are, but very engaging. The story has a serious side and will

resonate with many Aboriginal people, as well as anyone who has experienced dislocation and separation from family and community.

***The Lesser Blessed* by Richard Van Camp.**
A great, rambunctious, award winning wild romp with an unforgettable narrator. Larry Sole will remind you of every teenage guy you went to high school with, but at the same time, he's unlike anyone you've ever met. A character who's a real character!

***Monkey Beach* by Eden Robinson.**
Weird, dark, sometimes disturbing and beautifully written, this book was nominated for the Giller Prize.

***Green Grass, Running Water* by Thomas King.**
This novel was the most ambitious, complex novel yet by an Aboriginal writer coming out of Canada (if not exactly from Canada). To me, it represented a shift in form and structure and broadened the scope of Aboriginal fiction in Canada. It's well written, humorous and it introduced us to the Dead Dog Café.

THE INMATES ARE RUNNING THE ASYLUM

I have always been suspicious of political correctness –the imposition of a set of beliefs. Supposedly correct and socially conscious ones (though the water tends to get a bit muddy there) for the betterment of society. Some have even described the more radical forms as the new fascism. You could say they fall under the category of "seemed like a good idea at the time." Put that together with the naive enthusiasm of youth and strange things can happen in the name of that political correctness.

Such a thing has happened in a popular western university. In this far-off small university existed a theatre department, and in that theatre department existed a theatre professor. One of his responsibilities as part of the B.F.A. faculty theatre committee was to assist in deciding the following year's theatre season which would give the acting students some practical performing experience. As is often the situation in most acting classes, three quarters of the student body were female, necessitating programming of a play which largely consisted of female characters. As this professor often lamented, this meant repeated productions of plays like *Les Belles Soeurs* over the years. It seems few plays cater to such unique female casting situations. With this being said, the professor was understandably reluctant to program yet another production of *Lysistrata*, so he came up with a brilliant idea.

One of his personal favorites was a little play called *The Rez Sisters* by Tomson Highway. Granted all the characters were Native, but seven of the eight roles were female. Curious as to the reception of the idea, he pitched it to his theatre committee. They were concerned about the political implications of such a production, but were intrigued by the idea and suggested the Professor investigate further. He called a leading Native representative in the University to bounce the idea off of him. While this man of Aboriginal descent had some personal concerns about the play and felt it glorified bingo (which he considered to be just another form of on-Reserve gambling), he told the Professor to go ahead and gave his blessing. Next on the list was Tomson Highway, author of the play. Via email, Tomson gave more than his blessing; he congratulated the Professor for daring to go against common practice. Several months earlier, Highway wrote an

105

article for a journal rallying against artistic directors who were reluctant to produce *The Rez Sisters* and *Dry Lips Oughta Move To Kapuskasing* because they were afraid they might not be able to find enough Native actors to fill the roles. Highway believes non-traditional casting can work both ways and White people should have the option of playing Native people. The Professor was encouraged.

The only concern Highway expressed was when he was informed that the Professor had consulted a Native person at the University, with no background in theatre about the political viability of such a production. Highway responded with something to the effect of "If you were going to produce *Fiddler On The Roof*, would you consult your local Jew?" A good and logical point the Professor found hard to defend.

Armed with a thumbs-up from the author, and a secondary thumbs up from his colleague, the Professor told his students the wonderful news. He expected some positive response to his calculated and daring programming. Instead, many of the students were dismayed; some were downright uncomfortable with the idea. In the end, several individuals refused to audition for the play and the production was shut down a year before it was scheduled to because the students did not feel comfortable performing in a non-Native production of *The Rez Sisters*. They asked the Professor if they could do *Les Belles Soeurs* instead.

Now this is the irony of the situation: most Native actors I know, and after fifteen years in Native theatre and film I know a lot, live for the opportunity to play non-Natives. I've lost track of the times a Native friend has excitedly told me "I've got a part in a play/movie and guess what! I'm not playing an Indian!" Actors want to be hired for their talent, not their ethnicity. But that's a one way street. Most tragic of all, these poor students didn't realize that, this was probably the only time in their amateur and professional careers they would get the opportunity to portray a First Nations person. You think they would've jumped at the chance since a university production for educational and training reasons was conceivably their only shot at playing the 'skin game,' and they turned it down. Turns out they were uncomfortable with culturally appropriating those Aboriginal characters.

No doubt, sometime in their future they will gladly jump at the chance to play a child molester, a Nazi –a whole plethora of unsavory characters –with less thought they put into turning down this unique theatrical opportunity. As a Native person, I feel so privileged.

This also puzzled the Professor. The Professor inquired "You don't want to appropriate Native women, yet you are comfortable appropriating working class French Canadian woman." The answer was, "Yes but there are no French Canadians in (this western city), and there are lots of Native people here." I've heard the French never stray very far from their poutine and bagels.

In the end, neither *The Rez Sisters* nor *Les Belles Soeurs* were produced. The final result was the programming of *The Secret Rapture* by English playwright David Hare which has four female and two male roles. I have not read this particular play but have been assured by reputable sources that there are no Native characters in the play. So they should have had no problems.

TODAY IS A GOOD DAY TO GAMBLE

Remember the good old days when the media's perception of Native people leaned either towards a rather tragic or noble image, or of an alcoholic, or a land claim protester who could ride a horse bareback, while smudging an abandoned car on their front lawn with sweet-grass? I remember those days fondly because, as a Native person, I had the luxury, even the pleasure, of rising above those stereotypes to proudly declare to a prejudiced world, "I am not an alcoholic. I do not have a land claim. I cannot ride a horse, bareback or with a saddle." One was grateful for small victories.

My brethren and I have struggled to become more than just shallow images on international television so we proudly denounce pop culture's inaccurate impression of us as we drink our mochaccino lattes. In many ways it seems the perception, and misperception, of Native people (and other cultures) developed parallel to the creation of mass media. Several hundred years ago, a book consisting of letters written by Jesuits back to Europe detailing the life of Canada's Indigenous people was published. It was called *Relations*. It's on my shelf right next to W.P. Kinsella's *Born Indian*. Then came movies and television; and, there went the neighbourhood.

On a modern level, many of my Native actor friends constantly deal with preconceived notions which they are often asked to portray. They tell me of the "three question rule" they often had to face at auditions. First question – "Do you speak a Native language?" It was never, "Do you speak *YOUR* Native language?" Since most didn't care if a Cree spoke Haida or an Oneida spoke Inuktutuk, as long as it was a Native language. Second question –Befitting a noble warrior proudly surveying the limitless prairies, what do you look like without your shirt? Native actresses tend to find that one especially annoying. Third question was usually, "Can you ride a horse?" Since almost 70% of Native people live, or were brought up, in an urban environment, that one was always the hardest to fake. Still, most say they can. It's a matter of pride and a certain hope that something on a genetic level will kick in. Most seem to forget horses were introduced to North America only 400 years ago and have only been part of certain Aboriginal cultures for maybe three hundred of them. Actually, many Aboriginal cultures never had much use for horses, preferring to travel via rivers and lakes or other traditional methods. Technically, Caucasians have more of a genetic history with horses than Native people.

As a political statement, every time I'm in a bar I find myself asking every non-Native woman I meet if they speak their Indigenous language, what they look like without their shirt, and if they can ride a horse. Turn-about is fair play.

In the blink of an eye, there has arisen on the horizon a new Indian stereotype that has now become the most prominent perception our American neighbours have of Native people. I am talking about the connection between Casinos and Indians. On recent episodes of The West Wing, Family Guy, Son Of The Beach, and even The Simpsons to name a few, the only reference in the entire season (probably several seasons) to the First Nations of this continent was in some context with casinos.

In the April 8th, 2003 edition of PEOPLE magazine there is an article that reads "NATIVE SON: Harvard-educated entrepreneur Lance Morgan takes a gamble –and his Winnebago tribe hits the jackpot". Wading through the not so subliminal sub-text, you might be able to figure out what the article is about. Similarly, in the April 21st Internationally-syndicated Family Circus cartoon, Billy is telling his cowboy-dressed younger brother P.J., who is about to participate in a familiar children's game, "You be the cowboy, I'll be the Indian. I have a casino." I should mention Billy is dressed in a stylish tuxedo.

A few days ago while on a nostalgic whim, I leafed through a magazine I used to enjoy as a child –Mad Magazine. In a section called *Unconscious Racism*, was the line, "You see a Native American and you automatically assume he's got a piece of a casino somewhere." Last month I was in California where a friend admitted that most Californians didn't know there were Native people still living in their state until they started opening casinos a couple decades ago.

Casino Indians seem to be the new cliche in the media; one that has thrown most of the dark skinned original inhabitants of this land for a loop. Before we were proud to distance ourselves from those previous assumptions of the poor, oppressed images that we felt were beneath us because of the demeaning impression. To add insult to injury, many of my actor friends had finally gotten their angry, drunk, mystical, bare-back riding audition pieces down pat. Ironically, the tables have turned and everybody now expects us to be rich and successful. It's been a short hop going from blockading a road to setting up a casino, from wearing buckskin to a three piece suit, from paddling a canoe to driving a Lincoln. Somewhere in that process we seem to have missed the middle-class station. Do you see our dilemma?

Today, Native casinos are popping up here in Canada with alarming frequency, so it's only a matter of time until Canadians start developing that impresario impression too. Now the major twist arising from this issue is that this particular stereotype doesn't seem all that bad on the surface. A small part of me really wouldn't mind exploring this particular lifestyle. Maybe I do want a piece of a casino (so do many of my friends). Who am I to say the Americans are wrong? As long as they can back up their words. It's definitely a vertical move up the stereotype hierarchy. I have one slight problem though. The casinos up here seem to disagree. They won't return my calls. I might have to move to the States. Or, set up a casino in my apartment! I'm told I could do this since I heard on television that gambling is part of our traditional aboriginal way of life.

CURVE LAKE SPEECH

Ahneen. Tansi. Sago. Boozhoo. Welcome to wonderful downtown Curve Lake –my home and inspiration –deep in the heart of the Kawarthas. I always tell people Curve Lake is easy to find. Just go to the centre of the Universe and you're there.

I hope you've all had a hearty meal tonight because as luck would have it, I'm your dessert. Luckily for you I'm free-range, low fat and all you can eat. I better warn you though, in an hour you'll be hungry for me again.

My name is Drew Hayden Taylor. I was born and raised in this community, grew up just about a hundred yards in that direction. Then again, everything in Curve Lake is about a hundred yards in whatever direction. I used to go swimming at either the park or at Henry's. Baseball was over in that direction. Caught the bus for school over there. Cashed in my pop bottles to buy ice cream down that way. Went fishing at that end. Broke my uncle's window over there. There. Now you know just about everything you need to know about wonderful downtown Curve Lake. Granted it's a fairly small community; the population was only about 800 people when I lived here. But as I've been told many times, size doesn't matter. Does it, ladies?

Ask around and they'll tell you I'm Fritzie's boy –the kid that liked to read a lot. Not the worst reputation you can have in the world, because I've heard a lot worse. Don Kelly, an Ojibway speech writer for Matthew Coon Come and a stand-up comedian in Ottawa (now there's a surreal combination if I've ever heard one), says his Indian name is Runs Like A Girl. I guess nowadays mine would be something like "Writes Like A Post-modernist Aristotelian playwright from Curve Lake." To which most of you might respond, "Oh sure, like that narrows it down."

Many of you know me or my work. For those who don't, let me provide a little background for you. I'm a playwright, a journalist, a film maker, a scriptwriter, and, if I do say so myself, I make a darn good spaghetti sauce. As a writer, I have spent most of my life communicating. This is what a writer does. This is what I do. We writers manufacture ideas, give birth to stories, reinterpret reality, and practice communication. I think I can safely say it is the dream of every writer to someday... get it right. Or, at the very least, don't get it wrong.

I often refer to myself as a contemporary storyteller. I've heard other writers use the term "word warrior" or "weaver of words". Whatever the description used, it sure beats working for a living. I say that in jest because writing is extremely hard work and awesome in the effort. Trust me, there is no more frightening experience than looking at a blank computer screen with an equally blank imagination as the deadline ticks ever so near. Comes close to the experience of looking at a restless audience before opening night. That computer screen, ticking clock, and expectant faces have sent many a stronger man than me to tears. At least in other professions you can fake it. In accounting, you can fudge the numbers. If you're a Chief, you can blame it on someone else. But you can't hide in front of a blank screen or from an audience. An old axiom says that an audience can smell fear.

At the end of this terrifying yet creative journey there is a sense of accomplishment, of achievement, when what you are struggling to create is done. To look at a poster or a television program or a book and see your name upon it is a sensation which few come close to matching. You forget the pain and insecurity and say, "That wasn't so hard." I'm told childbirth is similar, but without the stretch marks. The great wit and writer Dorothy Parker once said, "I hate writing, but I love having written." Using that childbirth metaphor, "I hate writing, but I love having written" might explain the popularity of adoption. At least it is to my mother who takes great pleasure in reminding me that I was 11lb 12oz at birth. I wish I knew why women react so bizarrely when I mention that.

But I digress. As I said before, I am a playwright. Theatre is my life. My standard joke is I am married to theatre but have many mistresses. I have been fortunate and privileged to write a number of plays for young audiences, specifically young Native audiences. If the truth be told, I spent my first eighteen years in this place and this is where my creativity and inspiration originates. I never tell this to the Artistic Directors of the non-Native theatre companies who produced my plays. They might not appreciate my cultural nepotism. In the end, it's a small distinction because, as I'm sure you would agree, most children are alike regardless of which side of Cowboys and Indians they may play. My audiences, whether Native or non-Native, usually laugh where they're suppose to. There is a universality in being young that many of us lose as we get older. Since children share a commonality, why shouldn't their entertainment and education. One and one is still two whether you're Cree, Irish or Maori.

I am a true believer in the maxim that says true drama and comedy is universal. That is why many people today still enjoy four hundred year-old Shakespeare plays or twenty-five-hundred-year-old Greek tragedies. The fact that my plays take place in an environment, with an Aboriginal context and Aboriginal characters is irrelevant. Since they may add a few notes of familiarity for the kids to latch onto, but in the end it's usually the story or the emotion that kids relate to. Adults too, because as the cliche goes, there is no particular Native way to boil an egg. Thus, there is no particular Native way to fall in love, to get angry, or to be lonely... all universal traits of theatre.

That is why my plays have been produced over five dozen times across this country, in the States and in Europe. Think of it this way: of those five dozen productions, maybe one dozen were produced by a Native theatre company. That means my, and practically all, Aboriginal plays are cross cultural enough for a non-Native mainstream theatre company to spend between $50,000 and a $100,000 on each individual production. Let's face it, they don't do that unless they know they'll pull in a primarily non-Native audience.

As a Native playwright, just by sheer population representation, five-sixths of my audience have probably never been to a Reserve or ever had a car with rust spots. The point here is that, Native theatre is incredibly strong and powerful in Canada, laughably more than in the States. It survives on the interest and patronage of a Caucasian theatre-going audience. Native theatre is the darling of the middle class. Believe it or not, they can relate to our stories. So next time you hear a White person say, "I saw The Rez Sisters and it was simply wonderful. Wonderful! It made me take up bingo," go ahead and give them a hug.

Conversely, Native kids have many of the same feelings any other child has: they are afraid of monsters, and want to stay up past their bedtime. But, I could be all wrong since I'm not involved in Native education nor do I have kids... at least any that I know of. I've seen sufficient episodes of "7th Heaven" and "Dawson's Creek" to have a vague idea of what's going on.

By a weird quirk of irony I have dabbled extensively in the world of theatre for young audiences. Completely by accident too. I can assure you, I did not wake up one morning with a burning passion within me to write plays for young Native audiences. It just doesn't happen that way. Growing up here and going to school in Lakefield, I always believed theatre was about dead white people who talked funny.

My career in theatre happened because I just wanted to tell a good story. Plays for kids that I have written such as *Girl Who Loved Her Horses*, *The Boy in the Treehouse* and perhaps my most well known play, *Toronto at Dreamer's Rock,* have all explored the rocky world of Native youth. For *Toronto at Dreamer's Rock*, I won the prestigious Chalmer's Playwriting Award for Best New Play for Young Audiences. Not bad for my very first play. As a bonus, the prize included a cheque for $10,000 which I almost lost in a bar that night, but that's another story. Perhaps later.

Written in 1989, *Toronto at Dreamer's Rock* is my most successful play to date. It is rapidly approaching it's one millionth production this fall in Calgary. I refer to that play as my retirement fund because that simple one act play about three sixteen-year-old Odawa boys' search for identity has been produced in practically every part of Canada and in some States. It has been produced in Germany as a radio play and was published there with great success. God bless Germany and their love of all things Aboriginal. Das is goot. Ya.

Again it's that concept of universality being presented in a First Nations context. Three Native boys, one from four hundred years in the past, one from today, and one from a hundred years into the future, are dealing with the universal concept of identity. Who are we? Where do we fit in today's multifaceted and culturally diverse world? We've all traveled that dusty road to some degree. Rusty, Keesic and Michael are all Native (whatever that may mean), but they still ask questions about who they are and what it means to be Native. I have a sense that is a struggle you will find in most cultures.

It is always an interesting process when I sit down to write a play for young people. Many people make the mistake of thinking writing for kids is easy, downright simple in fact. People who believe or say this, are obviously not people who write for children, for a child's universe is just as complex and detailed as any one of you sitting out there. I acknowledge that I am probably preaching to the converted here, but us solitary writers have to keep that in mind when creating. Granted, there is an amazing amount of a willing suspension of disbelief in children –more so than in adults –but the story still has to be logical and make sense because children learn through familiarity. Which is to say that while a child's imagination may be vast and spectacular, it is confined within the world of reality. Their imagination is liquid, the bottle reality. Without that reality, the imagination would drip away. It would be a mess, might even be lost. At the risk of sounding like I'm repeating myself, that reality has to be real and understandable. Don't for a moment think it's an easy ride. Anything as important as a child's future shouldn't be. As a theatre artist, I know there is no tougher crowd than a room full of fidgety kids. If you don't grab and hold their attention immediately, it is lost permanently and the kids will wish they were off playing video games. Kids can be your best and your worst audience.

Working with young people is a constant, ongoing experiment that should never end. There are side benefits. Many an Elder told me it's their grandchildren that kept them young. Again, this not my area of expertise; but, I believe you can't do what I do without letting the child within you come out and play. In fact, it sometimes makes things a lot easier. Hell, I still watch Bugs Bunny, and at the tender age of forty, can't pass a large tree and wonder if I can make it to the top. The only difference between me and a big kid is, I'd bring a cooler with me.

You can find epiphany in the most unusual places. For instance, I found mine in the far northeast. I remember this one time I found myself in Labrador, the town of Goose Bay/Happy Valley to be specific. I was in the area as part of a larger arts festival the Board Of Education was holding in honour of John Cabot's "discovery" of Newfoundland several years back. Over three dozen artists ranging from illustrators to scientists to poets were there. Our only purpose was to visit the local and regional schools to expand children's minds. It was truly a fabulous idea. Since I was the only Native person invited, I was trotted out to show some cultural sensitivity. I was even sent up to Davis Inlet, several hours flight, for a two hour visit. It was a fascinating experience. In that small city of Goose Bay I learned something new about kids and my own personal interrelation with them. During the week there, all the artists visited several schools during their stay to maximize the potential of their visit. One day alone I visited five classes and pretty much after talking about yourself and what you do for over five hours for five days, you can get pretty bored with yourself. At least I did... and I'm sure that will be news to my family.

Before I arrived, I had requested that I be limited to the older classes, grade eight and up, for two reasons. The first being I wasn't sure if the younger kids would understand theatre theory. Brechtian and Aristotelean drama might not combine well with Dr. Seuss or Harry Potter. Secondly, I don't really know what makes kids that young, tick. I'm a single child of a single parent. Most of my previous interaction with children was limited to elbowing my way through McDonald's to get a decent toy in my McHappy meal.

So there I am, in the wilds of Labrador after being picked up at the airport by one of the coordinators. As I'm being driven to the festival office, this particular gentleman handed me my lecture schedule. At least a third of the twenty or so lectures I was scheduled to give were to kindergarten and grades one and two. Somewhere deep inside my body seized up. I reminded them of my request and they said something to the effect that I had been in such high demand, that they wanted to make the best use of my time there. I'm afraid that didn't help much.

I confessed my uncertainty about the situation and he shrugged it off saying, "Oh just play some theatre games with them. They'll have fun with that." My response was, "Okay, what are theatre games?" He gave me a shocked double take. Famed playwright doesn't know what theatre games are? What do I know about theatre games? I'd heard of them. I am a playwright. I sit in my office alone and make things up. It's kind of hard to play theatre games with my plants. Theatre games! I was screwed.

My first class of ankle biters wasn't until the next morning, so for most of the night I was scared. I tossed and turned, trying to figure out what to do. What did I know about five, six, seven year-olds other than they can swarm like bees when bored or upset. When you're in Labrador in the middle of winter and the Festival has your return plane ticket and you don't get paid until you leave, your options are very limited. It looked like I would have to do this.

Now this may not sound like much of a dilemma to you guys, but please keep in mind I find lecturing to people who are interested in what I do, trying at the best of times. Talking to young kids was a terrifying concept. You guys do this for a living and get paid huge sums of money I'm sure, but a writer such as myself lives a solitary life. Just me, a computer and whatever imagination I can muster. You'll notice there are no lectures to cookie grabbers mentioned in that sentence. I make it a rule not to associate with people I can't go drinking with and I understand that's frowned upon at most primary schools.

So there I am, at this primary school early the next day and it's show time (as we say in my business). I am ushered into a room with approximately twenty to twenty-five future citizens of Canada, all sitting at their thigh-high desks. It was a scene straight out of Kindergarten Cop. At least Schwarzenegger had a gun. The kids were all looking at me with curiosity and their restlessness was evident. Like they were thinking, *who is this guy and why is he here talking to us? Doesn't he know there's playdough to be eaten?* I am introduced and manage to make it to the front of the class to start explaining who I am and what I do in as simple terms as possible. I had written a couple of episodes of two children's series for television titled 'The Longhouse Tales' and 'Prairie Berry Pie' and a handful of plays by that time, so I figured those writings gave me a crash course in how to relate. That feeling was rapidly evaporating.

If anybody ever doubted the existence of a patron saint of public speaking, have doubts no longer, for on that day in the far off northeast, I was blessed. Out of nowhere came a voice and an idea... or more accurately a salvation... and I was saved. Yeeaaahhh! Earlier that year, I toyed with an idea of writing a children's story or play about a young girl who had a monster hiding in her closet. She was terrified of it. Only this monster didn't want to be a monster, he wanted to be a dentist; but all the dentist positions were filled, and the only job available at the moment was a monster position.

The problem was the monster didn't know anything about being a monster. He could do a pretty decent root canal, but he didn't know a darned thing about scaring little girls, which was supposed to be his job. He wasn't very effective as a monster. He was actually pretty pathetic. In the story (as much of it as I'd bothered to develop before getting distracted), the little girl ended up feeling sorry for him and decided to teach him how to be a good and effective monster. She learned to not be afraid of monsters and he developed a friend.

Armed with that background, I had a brainstorm. I would ask these kids for help in developing this story. I told them I didn't know much about little girls or monsters either, so I was in a bit of a pickle. If they didn't mind, would they help me write the play. Well, I have never, in my life seen a flood of hands reach for the sky, especially when I asked, "What do you think the monster would look like?" Every student had an opinion and definitely wanted to be heard. I followed up with additional questions. "What does a monster sound like?" "What should the little girl call him?" "What's the little girl's name?" For each question I asked, I got at least two or three responses *per* student. It was wonderful. The kids didn't want me to leave when the class was over.

That was the revelation I received from kids I'd been fearing and dreading. I'd never seen such active, interested, excited faces. This is probably old hat to all of you, but it was a major discovery for me. When you have the attention of a child, they are completely and totally in your universe. They give with their heart and soul. I was amazed. These kids couldn't help quickly enough, so I ended up being as excited as them. It worked in all the other classes too. My adult-elitist butt was saved and I, not just the students, had learned something too.

The point of this little anecdote is to remind myself why I, a forty-year-old man with no children, continue to write plays and television shows for children. It is because every once in a while, I tap into the child within me. I learn something. In one of my adult plays, oddly enough called *Only Drunks and Children Tell the Truth*, I wrote a line about White people trying to tap into their inner child, while Native people try to tap into their inner Elder. I may have to revise that. Each passing day brings me closer to my inner... and outer Elder, and farther from that inner child. I find myself longing for my childhood days.

Here I am in the place I spent most of those days where much of the inspiration for my writings comes from. I proudly say that I went to Mud Lake Indian Day School for grades one and two... about a hundred yards in that direction. After that auspicious beginning, I was bussed to Lakefield from grades three up till grade twelve. At an early age I made a surprising discovery. You could learn as many interesting things on the bus as you do in class. Some things are more important. I figured, I spent approximately 1,300 hours of my life either waiting for that school bus to pick me (and everybody else) up or riding in it. That's almost two straight months of existence around a stupid yellow bus. And to think, I could have spent that time eating playdough.

My very first school is now part of the village day care... a hundred yards in that direction. The school I went to in Lakefield was torn down about twenty years ago and the intermediate school I went to is now the junior school. When did all this happen? When did I get so old? All the kids I remember playing with, teasing, hiding on, now have kids of their own. I've partied with these kids who have grown up to have kids. I have a cousin, who's two days older than me and has been a grandfather for several years now. Maybe I *won't* be climbing any more trees after all. Maybe I have found my inner Elder. As proof, people seem to think I know things now. Silly people.

I find myself lecturing at my third conference on Native childhood education with my only qualification that I was once a Native child. Silly people. The first such conference was in Whistler about five years ago, the second in Saskatoon about three years ago and now one in my own backyard. As much as it frightens me, I think this officially means I am no longer one of us, I am one of them. And so are all of you. In this world of taking sides, we are all "them" –the authority, the establishment, sources of information and allowance. We have grown to be our parents.

To use a cliche, it seems yesterday when I was learning to read. I distinctly remember my mother bringing comic books home for me when I was around four or five. I loved the vivid pictures and bold designs, not to mention all these strange white people in even stranger costumes. That was an added bonus. Now I live in Downtown Toronto, with even stranger white people in even stranger costumes. But I digress. Eventually I had a whole stack of comic books when my mother and I lived in the *Old House*... about a hundred yards in that direction. We lived there until I was about six, when we moved to a new house across from my grandparents. The house is no longer new, about 35 years old. (Notice that age thing creeping in again?) I have definitely got to stop doing these childhood conferences. They make me too reflective.

Anyway, I remember looking repeatedly through all these comic books at all the exciting images, and thinking "I can't wait to learn to read so I can figure out what all these people are doing and saying."

Even back then, I knew what wonderful doors reading would open for me. I knew it could take me to places the pictures couldn't. How ironic that several decades later I became a writer. I haven't written a comic book yet; but hope is eternal. Then I will have come full circle. Even my beloved grandparents thought I read way too much and once urged my mother to not let me read so much. They thought it wasn't right. This is probably one of the only things I did, and still do, to openly disobey the words of my grandparents. I'm too old to retrain.

Maybe our uncomfortable relationship with reading has something to do with the fact we all come from a traditionally oral culture. Our belief systems, our stories, our histories were all passed down by word of mouth for generations. Admittedly, I do find it ironic that I and many other Native authors, make our living from this thing known as literature or the written word. As a result, we are becoming less and less oral. I am reminded of the words of the novelist James Joyce who wrote "I am forced to write in a conquerors tongue" as he reflected Britain's control of his native Ireland and their suppression of the Irish language. This can be said of the Native literary world I'm afraid to say. And it has continued onto the next logical stage. What was once an oral culture, currently dabbling with the literary world, has basically become a media universe as television, cd's and computers all run our reserves and the world. In the end, a good story will still be a good story in whatever form it takes. A child is still a child regardless of technology. So our little ones don't play with Tonka toys as much anymore, they surf the net. Instead of listening to stories around the campfire, they watch the Star Wars series. Kraft dinner has replaced moose meat. When I was a kid, there was one universal factor in the over 600 Aboriginal communities in Canada, that being Country music. It seemed nearly everybody from Eel Ground, New Brunswick to Squamish, British Columbia could quote Hank Williams better than the Bible. Is it still true, I wonder?

Times change and so do we. In a few hundred years, we've gone from wearing buckskin to bell bottoms and now thongs. You know who you are. Deep down inside we all know who we are and what is important. To quote that classic of Native themed musical nostalgia from Paul Revere and the Raiders who put it best when they sang, "Though I wear a shirt and tie, I'm still a Redman deep inside." Indian

Reservation from the late Sixties. If I can quote from that song, boy I really am getting old.

Education for our children is pretty high on the list of things we must pay attention to. Damn near the top I would say. Teaching children everything they need to know about surviving in this technologically dominant world is extremely important. The world is changing faster than we can keep up with it. It's been said you can't teach an old dog new tricks. I don't believe that and I don't think you do. Equally important, as vitally important is teaching their past and the beliefs, language and history of their people. Unless you know where you're coming from, how can you know where you're going. Your responsibility is to teach new dogs –the children –old tricks, or traditions.

Responsibility. It's an interesting word. Just a few weeks ago, I heard a Native politician, of all people, say that being Native, Aboriginal, First Nations, Indigenous or whatever the politically correct term of the day might be, is neither a right nor a privilege, but a responsibility. With obligations and duties. One is to look after our future generations and God bless anybody who dares to take that on in a formal manner. Even if it isn't your official job, it is still your blessing and your honour to hold their hand and help them count the fingers on that hand. Indeed, it is your responsibility to provide the flashlight to show the way through the darkness of the future. Anything to do with children –having them, feeding them, teaching them –is definitely more of a responsibility than a right or privilege. A right or privilege takes the onus off us and puts it onto other people. Responsibility gives us direction. We need to keep that in mind.

Boy, for somebody who says he knows nothing about Native childhood education, I sure can preach a lot, can't I? And weirder, I sound like I almost know what I'm talking about. The beauty of being a writer is you can talk about almost anything you want and people will believe you. You should hear my lecture on nuclear physics. Please take everything I say with a grain of sand... I'm making most of it up anyways. It's the trickster in me; but since the Trickster is a symbol of everything we do, right as well as wrong, maybe I'm not making anything up. As we all know, truth is truly stranger than fiction and supposedly will set us free.

So we've come to the end of a long hard day, and it was your turn to be a student today. Hopefully you have learned many fine things which you will take to your communities. I will leave tonight knowing the three elements that make up our unique Aboriginal reality have been fully stated today. Mind, body and spirit. Workshops, dinner and me. Now that is indeed a full day. I hope I have not bored you with my humble ramblings, but if so, blame Dixie. She hired me. Like a good Ojibway man, I just do what a woman tells me to.

Before I go, I'd like to leave you with some words of wisdom I found in the Native and non-Native worlds. I believe they encapsulize everything we are here to achieve and everything we believe in. The American author and scientist Benjamin Franklin (you may have heard of him) said over two hundred years ago, "If a man empties his purse into his head, no man can take it from him. An investment in knowledge always pays the best interest." I agree. All the money spent on education is not a waste. Any money cut from education, is a loss now and in the future.

Red Cloud, a proud Sioux Chief in the late 19th century, was negotiating for his people with a group of White men. Explaining their position, he said "I am poor and naked, but I am the chief of the nation. We do not want riches but we do want to train our children right..."

We do not want riches, but we do want to train our children right, was said 130 years ago. Today, very little difference. Truth knows no calender. Carry on your most excellent work.

This has truly been a pleasure for me and I hope it has been for you too. Thank you for coming to this lovely little spot in the world and for putting up with me. And if anybody asks, you never saw me here. Thank you. *Ch'meegwetch.*

MY BIG BREAK

I'm sitting in a car in a deserted parking lot in Toronto's east end at 5:00 a.m. on a freezing cold Canadian winter morning. To top it off, I'm covered in blood. I've just said to a hooker, "Okay, you can get out of my car now, bitch" after partaking of her unique talents. The lady of questionable virtue has registered her disapproval of my rather graphic order by twice plunging a large knife into my chest. This scenario is repeated almost a dozen times more before the director yells "cut." Then, go home and like King Lear and Pontius Pilate try to wash the fake blood from my hands and body. So much for my big film debut.

The lady with the short temper and a fondness for cutlery is Jennifer Podemski, actress and producer with Big Soul Productions, an Aboriginal production company she operates along with Laura Milliken in Toronto. This is the first night of shooting for an edgy half-hour drama titled *Laurel* written by Patrick Tenascon and directed by Craig Bernard. Jennifer plays the central character, a disgruntled streetwalker with severe personal issues which results in a magnificent death scene from yours truly.

Prior to this, Big Soul Productions' claim to fame was a highly successful profile series on the Aboriginal Peoples Television Network called The Seventh Generation. This series is about to enter its third season. The mandate of the show is to introduce, interview and highlight the fabulous things being done by young people in the Native communities. Big Soul Productions decided to try their hand at something a little more dramatic and came up with *Laurel*.

With an almost entirely Aboriginal cast and crew, this show is another sign of the growing maturity of the Native film and video industry. Approximately 75% of the cast and crew were Native, ranging from the grips, to the makeup artists, to the gaffers.

I was probably the only amateur participating in the production. I have always been content to be a writer. Prior to this little adventure, the most acting I'd ever done was in singles bars. (My acting resume consisted of being an inconsequential extra on a Cher movie, two Public Service Announcements, and a small part in a television series called *Spirit Bay*.) This was my first speaking role and my line "Okay, you can get out of my car now, bitch!" was not exactly, "It is the

Winter of our discontent made glorious etc..." However, the line conveyed emotion, transmitted an action, and provided a certain amount of character. There are no small parts, only small actors. This is where I come in, for they don't come any smaller than me.

Being a low budget production, Jennifer and Laura called in a few favours and provided a unique opportunity for friends to have cameos in their labour of love. Jennifer, known for her performance work in the movies like *Dance Me Outside* and television series *The Rez* and *Riverdale*, asked if I was interested in playing a sleazy john. I admit that isn't an opportunity that pops up too frequently in my life, so I jumped at it. I can do sleazy; which is why I ended up in that parking lot at that godforsaken hour –and on Valentine's Day to boot.

It was a family affair for Jennifer: her mother provided the craft services (like catering): and her boyfriend was the camera operator. It's no wonder between takes of the simulated sex in the front seat of the car, Jennifer took the time to yell to her boyfriend, "I love you," and occasionally mutter to me, "I can't believe my mother is watching this!" I, as the soon to be dead john, just sat there wondering if I should say my one and only line with an Irish French, or Cree accent. Having a beautiful woman straddle you in a car, then jump up and down repeatedly, can certainly play havoc with your concentration. I decided to go with the Curve Lake Ojibway accent, nuances which I had mastered long ago as a child.

I ended up being driven home at 7:30 that morning, twelve and a half hours after I'd been called to the set. I seem to remember being told I'd be home by midnight at the latest. I was exhausted, frozen to the core from spending three and a half hours covered in cold, wet fake blood in minus ten degree weather. I was in a red 1990 Honda Accord instead of the limo I had envisioned. I was not happy.

...I can't wait to do it again!

NAKED CAME THE INDIAN —ABORIGINAL EROTICA IN THE 21ST CENTURY

"Indigenous Erotica is political. More than that, it's stimulating, inspiring, beautiful, sometimes explicit. It's written by Indigenous writers, painted by Indigenous painters, filmed by Indigenous film makers, photographed by Indigenous photographers, sung by Indigenous singers."

"Erotica, Indigenous Style," Kateri Akiwenzie-Damm

As a child I remember being told Nanabush legends. Legends are often the souls of a culture. Tales of silliness, adventure, and those with moral and philosophical implications. More than once, I distinctly remember hearing stories of a more scatological or bawdy nature. Tales which had that randy Trickster from Ojibway mythology chasing women and sometimes men. Through his own insatiable sexual appetites, Nanabush created some unique erotic mischief. Nanabush is often referred to as representing the best in humanity and the worst in humanity. Often, there's no better way of investigating a nation than through their amorous adventures.

In Native communities of this country, the perception and practice of sex has gone through an amazing and, at times, tragic metamorphosis in the five hundred plus years since immigration opened. Keep in mind that there were approximately 53 distinct languages and dialects, each belonging to a unique culture, at point of contact. Through no fault of our own, every one of those diverse people's perception and practice of sexuality have been affected by colonization. Only within the last generation have Native people, mostly artists, been examining Aboriginal sexuality in its past, present and future forms.

Before contact, in what I call "The Before Time", there was a healthy and practical view of sexuality. Due to weather and available resources, many cultures often had large families with generations living under a communal roof. Privacy was a foreign concept so the act of sex was no secret, and was seen as a common occurrence. As a result, childhood awareness of sexuality began at an early age. Sex was not something to be feared or hidden but was viewed as a natural part of life.

As I stated earlier, many traditional legends of the Trickster and other generic legends often had sex as a focus because, like everything in the natural world, it was entertaining, funny, and part of everyday life. Nearly every Native person who could read or has a libido, has either bought, borrowed or stole the book, *Tales From the Smoke House*, written by Herbert T Schwartz and illustrated by Daphne Odjig. Published in the late 1960's, the book features a collection of erotic legends from various Nations. The initial response was predictable. "Wow, Indians have sex?" This book provided yet another portal from which the general public viewed Native people and their legends. No longer were our stories seen as amusing children's stories. We also had stories of teachings for all ages.

On a more practical front, direct sex education of the younger generation began, often with family members taking charge of the instruction. It was the common practice in the Iroquois culture (and many others) for a close relative, usually an aunt or uncle, to take a young boy or girl aside at the proper time to talk about the proverbial birds and bees and, more importantly, the responsibilities involved in the act of sex. It was not something to be embarrassed about, but something to be responsible with.

Sex and its effect on culture were often in the forefront of a lot of traditional art. Various works of art at Toronto's Royal Ontario Museum, Ottawa's Museum of Civilization and other such collections reflect that freedom and convey a wide selection of erotic expressions. Phallic rattles, passionate Inuit and various other carvings attest to a traditional connection with sexuality.

Oddly enough, with the advent of interest in traditional Inuit art, most of the politically incorrect carvings were forced underground. During the middle part of this century, when the Church held sway in those communities, and art dealers from the south who came looking for Inuit art, both groups frowned upon the more explicit carvings. Dealers feared they might limit the resale value in the more conservative south. As a result, many sexually based carvings ended up being sold to miners, construction workers and sailors, with very little reaching the larger galleries. It seemed to the Inuit carvers, there was a smaller market for erotic carvings so logically they concentrated on the more lucrative pieces.

This was one of the many influences the Church exerted over Native sexuality and other cultural practices. The meeting of these two divergent ways of life left monumental lasting scars on the Aboriginal psyche that are still in the healing process, centuries after the first incidents. Then into the Native world of open and healthy sexuality, appeared European paternalism and the Church. Priests, missionaries and other foreigners, with different beliefs and contradictory ideas swept across the land. They came to Aboriginal communities to teach the gospels of God, dictating "thou shalt not acknowledge thy body." It appeared as though they didn't want Native people to have sex and that they shouldn't talk about sex, let alone enjoy it. Sex wasn't for fun – but for reproduction. Sex became evil. Sex and its many representations went underground.

Perhaps realizing the message their missionaries were preaching had limited results in this immense country, they did the best thing they could. If the mountain won't come to Mohammed, then send Mohammed to the mountain. Like pneumonia following a bad cold, the Residential schools came next, with their own skewed belief in the practice of sex. Sexual abuse became rampant and the counteractive philosophy of "Do as I say, not as I do" took on tragic consequences.

The residential school system was an agreement created between the Federal Government and various churches, primarily Catholic and Anglican, to share responsibility for educating the Indigenous people of this land. To save money huge buildings were built in strategic locations across the country. Thousands of children were huddled together in planes and trains and sent, often for twelve years at a time. Thousands of Mohammeds went to the mountains. Ironically, this deal made in Hell sealed the fate of several generations of Native children and like a sickness, it was also communicable.

Abuse became cyclical, passed down over generations and resulting in a damaged consciousness and wounded psyches. Several surveys report that in some Native communities, as many as six out of ten Native women have been sexually abused. Perhaps nowhere is this distortion of sexual understanding better illustrated than through the homophobia that grips many of our communities today. Once, Two-Spirited people were given places of privilege, often as Medicine people had. Their contribution to the community was honoured, not reviled.

That being said, new winds are blowing. Like a breath of fresh air, there seems to be a resurgence of interest and pride in redefining what Aboriginal sexuality is. Many argue it never really died, but went underground to places where the dominant society couldn't find and destroy it. For example, Métis writer Maria Campbell has often told me how intrinsically saucy the Cree language is. What is normally an uninteresting sentence in English comes to life in some risque manner when translated to Cree. I've heard the same said about other Aboriginal tongues.

As with the traditional dances, songs and languages, our sexual belief system refused to die out. Legends kept it alive. As history shows, stories are very hard to kill. The tales were merely waiting for a new generation of people to explore and reclaim their sexuality. In the late 1800's, Louis Riel said, "My people will go to sleep for a hundred years and it will be the artists that will wake them up." Who better than artists to explore the issue and revitalize it. Artists from many different disciplines have heard the cultural alarm clock go off and have eagerly set out to reclaim what is ours.

Several years ago, an art exhibit (called EXPOSED) toured Regina, Ottawa, and Brantford. The exhibit featured erotic visual and installation art by First Nations artists from across Canada. Rosalie Favel, Norval Morrisseau, Thirza Cuthand and Daphne Odjig, to name a few, were all represented for the first show of this kind. There have been other memorable artistic explorations. Poets like Kateri Akiwenzie-Damm, Marilyn Dumont, and Greg Scofield have pushed the boundaries of erotic writing for years now.

Theatre, one of the best barometers of what's on the mind of the people, has long been critical of the sexual abuse which plague our society. It seemed like practically every Native play written over the last fifteen years has made reference to rape, prostitution or some form of sexual exploitation, notably *The Rez Sisters* and *Drylips Oughta Move to Kapuskasing* by Tomson Highway, *fareWell* by Ian Ross, *MoonLodge* by Margo Kane, *Princess Pocahontas and The Blue Spots* by Monique Mojica to name a few.

During this transition phase, different philosophies about what is or isn't appropriate tended to bump heads. Consider the concept of "cultural hypocrisy." Somewhere in Saskatoon is a grandmother, who prefers to remain nameless but, suffice it to say, she frequents many pow wows and ceremonies. She's a very hip and sexy lady who has been told several times to leave Aboriginal ceremonies because she favours skirts that are knee-length, not the more respectable and required ankle length. She finds this frustrating because many Elders she's talked with had no problem with a bare ankle; it's that middle generation who've been taught to cover up and hide their bodies. Some would argue this is a fallout from the Christian sexual myopia.

One of the more difficult aspects of researching this issue is trying to determine what can actually be classified as Native erotica in terms of today. Back in "The Before Time" there was no pop culture other than our everyday lives. Today, mainstream industries and the dominant culture have altered what was once easily identified as ours. They have even appropriated aspects of our culture into theirs, while trading back dubious examples of their own sexuality.

In theory, I tend to discount First Nation exotic dancers as legitimate expressions of Aboriginal sexuality. As long as the girl is pretty and shapely, I don't think patrons of these establishments look above the collar bone to see what nationality the dancer is, or are interested in a frank discussion of cultural issues. I could be wrong and if any dancer would like to talk me out of that opinion, I'm willing to listen.

However, male dancers are horses of a different colour. They tend to use themes and characters in their performance such as a cop, a fireman and so on. I've heard it argued that women prefer a narrative, more context while men, don't feel the need for such unnecessary details. I found one Native male dancer in Mississauga, Ontario who entertained the ladies dressed as an Indian Brave. Granted, that's an admittedly grey area.

I found two porn films with the titles "Poca-ho-ass" and "Ger-anal-mo". For obvious reasons, I don't think these films are accurate or valid reclamations of our sexuality. Also, somewhere in cyberspace is a web site devoted to nude native Americans. "We are a beautiful people" reads the promotion. I agree, although that might not be the best venue for arguing the case.

My aim, with all this research, is to produce a documentary on Native Erotica for the National Film Board of Canada. There are many interesting issues to be debated on this subject, I've only revealed the proverbial tip of the iceberg. It's a complex and controversial topic. As usual, everyone will have an opinion. What do you think Aboriginal erotica is? What does reclaiming our sexuality involve?

A SPACE HAS BEEN RESERVED FOR US

It's no secret that within the last twenty years growth in First Nations literature is impressive and voluminous. Native authors such at Lee Maracle, Tomson Highway, Jeannette Armstrong, Tom King and Basil Johnston have flooded our nation's book stores with a surprising quantity and quality of writings. Years ago, Canada's premiere Native theatre company, Native Earth Performing Arts had to beat the proverbial bushes in a search of enough Aboriginal playwrights to participate in the first annual Weesageechak Begins to Dance Playwright's Festival back in June of 1989. Today, nearly every major theatre company in Canada has produced at last one Native play. More importantly, these same companies have committed to developing new Aboriginal stories and plays. While still at the forefront of Native theatre development, Native Earth Performing Arts is no longer the only game in town.

Not surprisingly, more than Native theatre is exploding. Native literature and its practitioners are increasingly visible on the Festival circuit. This summer alone, I was lucky enough to be invited to Italy's Turin International Book Fair, the Lakefield Literary Festival, and the Eden Mills Authors Festival. In this acknowledgement of our voice, I noticed a surprising trend at some of these author's festivals. A trend which, on the surface, hints at a unique form of literary segregation, however unintentional.

A few months ago in Lakefield, I and two other writers were programmed for an afternoon slot called "First Nations Writers: Then and Now." The readers consisted of myself, Kateri-Akiwenzie Damm and the well known biographer Charlotte Gray, who to the best of my knowledge is not Native, but had written an excellent book called Flint & Feather: The Life and Times of E. Pauline Johnson, Tekahionwake, which detailed the life of the Mohawk poet. I'm guessing that gave Gray the necessary credentials for the day. Last month, I was invited to read at the Eden Mills Author's Festival outside of Guelph, along with Tom King and several other Aboriginal writers. We were scheduled to read in the "Aboriginal Area", although I believe Tom King did manage an appearance in one of the mainstream tents. A non-Native friend who attended our readings commented that his first thought on seeing the "Aboriginal Area" sign was that it suggested a sense of marginalization.

After attending these two events, I couldn't help but wonder aloud whether being apart was necessarily a good thing. I do acknowledge what a confusing issue it is. I enjoy and look forward to reading and participating with my Aboriginal brother and sister writers since we share many of the same origins and inspirations. Keeping that in mind, are we ghettoizing ourselves or allowing ourselves to be ghettoized? The noteworthy George Elliot Clarke, one of Canada's leading Black poets and authors, was also at Eden Mills, but I don't remember seeing an "Afro-Canadian Area." In a conversation we had some time back, Clarke acknowledged some Mi'kmaq blood from his Nova Scotia ancestors. Maybe he should have read with us.

Please don't get me wrong, I'm not being critical or judgmental of these festivals. As an author I am damn glad to be invited anywhere literature (Native and non-Native) is celebrated. I was taught from a young age that a guest should never criticize their host. Both festivals were fabulously run and a lot of fun. We were treated very well and I came away with good memories and new friends. In fact, it was my third trip to the Lakefield Festival. I hope to be invited back to both festivals again and again. I should also point out the Eden Mills "Aboriginal Area" was conceived by the town's First Nation residents, who wanted to highlight and honour the First Nation voice and words. As I said, the question gets complicated and so are the answers.

Several years ago I was asked to read at the famous Toronto International Authors Festival. I opened for American author E. L. Doctrow who, I'm fairly certain, has no noticeable tribal or Native affiliation (I could be wrong). I was just another writer hanging out with a couple other writers, feeling like a grown-up author ready to compete with the world's best. To this day, I've been meaning to read one of E. L. Doctrow's books.

The perception of Native people in the writing world is becoming even more complex. Not long ago, we were a tragically oppressed, depressed and suppressed minority struggling to reclaim our voice. Contracts were put on W.P Kinsella and woe to the non-Native person who dared to write a story in an Aboriginal context. Now, the definition, or perhaps a better word is categorization, of the Native voice is a difficult task.

On October 5th, as part of this years Weesageechak Begins To Dance Festival, Native Earth is holding a Native Playwright's Symposium. I and several First Nation's playwrights will participate in a panel discussion titled "Dances With Mainstream", that deals with getting the Aboriginal voice into the dominant culture. When that panel is over, I have to catch a bus to Peterborough where I have been asked to sit on a panel discussion put together by PEN CANADA, an organization that champions oppressed writers around the world. This panel is titled "Splitting Heres: Literary Elucidations of Exile, Refuge, Voice and Identity".. If I understand this correctly, in the morning, I am going to be mainstream and a couple of hours later, and a hundred kilometers away, I will be oppressed again.

How do you dress for things like this? Just make sure your Dorothy Grant (a very talented and successful Haida designer in Vancouver) shirt wasn't made in a Filipino sweatshop... or in a Nanaimo one.

Yay-ees and Ya-aas
(My mother's way of saying thingamajigs and whatcha-ma-call-its)

INGINS AMONG US

And now for something a little different:

Several years ago, I was asked by CAM, the Centre for Aboriginal Media, to write a Public Service Announcement about racism that would air on television. They had purchased some stock footage of Indians attacking a wagon train and urged me to consider using it. I thought about it for a while; banging my head against a wall; pacing back and forth in my house; praying to every Creator I could think of, for inspiration. I don't normally take contracts like this because for me it's difficult enough to come up with an original idea by itself, so to develop something with strings attached was even more cumbersome. Finally, I had an idea, and this is the result.

It turned out to be one of those projects that was really fun to do (I did not use their footage though.) The more I saw it, the prouder I became of it. One person told me it was one of the smartest things I ever wrote. Because of that compliment, I'm almost impossible to live with now.

INGINS AMONG US

Fade up on a young Aboriginal couple ensconced comfortably in theatre chairs, munching on popcorn and watching a conventional cowboys and Indian movie.

On the screen they couple is watching a movie with an Indian war party and cavalry fighting it out. The woman, who is disgusted by the movie, leans over to the man and whispers.

WOMAN:
Wouldn't it be nice to see one of these things be a little bit accurate?

The man smiles in agreement.

Meanwhile, on the screen the scene changes and a war party of young warriors ride up to their Chief who is waiting on a bluff, overlooking a slow-moving wagon train. They wait for him to speak. After surveying the vulnerable settlers, he speaks majestically to his warriors.

CHIEF:
They come, like ants to a dead dog. We will attack and take many scalps.

One inquisitive warrior raises his hand for a question.

WARRIOR # 1:
Un... excuse me. But I was talking to my grandfather last night and he doesn't know anything about this scalping thing. It was news to him.

CHIEF:
Well... umm.. you see...

WARRIOR # 2:
Yeah, what's up with that?

Another warrior shifts uncomfortably on his horse.

WARRIOR # 3:
And will someone tell me why I'm on this horse. I'm Mohawk, man, we never had horses. Can somebody get me off this thing? Do they bite? Huh? Do they?

Another warrior interrupts.

WARRIOR # 4:
And has anybody else noticed it's freezing out here and we're all sitting around in buckskin loincloths?

WARRIOR # 2:
Yeah, what's up with that?

CHIEF:
Many good questions you have...

WARRIOR # 4:
Hey man, do you realize that your verbiage is constantly full of syntax errors. Man, what university did you go to?

CHIEF:
Hey, get off my back, I'm not even Native, I'm Italian... but I needed the work.

All the other warriors turn their horses to leave, muttering to themselves.

VARIOUS WARRIORS:
Oh well then...
I wonder if he's related to Columbus...
Help, my horse is moving...
Anybody up for some basketball, I think I saw a hoop on that last covered wagon.

Cut back to the couple on the couch.

WOMAN:
I love happy endings.

The screen fades to white as the billboard comes up to say:
SEE PEOPLE FOR WHO THEY REALLY ARE

Fade To Black.

BURNING QUESTIONS OF EXISTENCE

One of the great things about being a published author and playwright is that I get to travel the world to do readings and lectures in amazing places where I meet lots of fascinating people. It's a position most would envy –I know I would if I wasn't doing it. A drawback to this scenario (and it's a minor one), is the tiresome repetitive questions I'm asked after a public reading. I truly don't mean to sound ungrateful, but when you answer the same question once or twice a month for fifteen years in places ranging from Italy and Germany, to Kelowna and Prince Rupert, the novelty wears off... if you know what I mean.

Granted, there's no way a high school student in Edmonton will know that I answered their question on the Mohegan Reservation in Connecticut just eight days before, and at the University of Brussels in Belgium a scant three months earlier and in Eureka, California two years before that, and three dozen places in between. Global village, my ass!

I acknowledge that these same people may buy my books (what with Native theatre such a popular seller) and prove to my mother that, yes indeed, I do have a job. And often it's their tax money that is indirectly being rerouted into my wallet via reading fees. So, please understand that I feel somewhat guilty in offering this trifling criticism. In comparison, it's like one of the drawbacks of being a food critic is you sometimes tend to put on weight. Now, in the spirit of economy and to kill several birds with one stone, I offer up a distilled version of popular questions I frequently get asked, complete with answers. These have been gleaned from hours and hours of question and answer sessions, which, I actually love doing. Other than the Jerry Springer show, where else will I get a room full of people eager to see what I'm going to say and do. Be warned though, sometimes I like to play with my audience and have included some of my more playful answers (as well as the real ones.) I'll leave it up to you to figure out which is which, I can't give away all my secrets.

Q. Where do you get your ideas?

Most of them come from that week I spent doing acid in a Venezuelan bordello. (I once gave this answer at a press conference in State College, Pennsylvania, the Amish capital of that state, then realized the Amish aren't really into either acid or Venezuelan bordellos.)

Q. What's your most favorite book/play/article you've written?

I've always found this to be an unfair question. It's like asking who is your favorite child? Each one is special, unique, and came from a sacred source. And I've written television shows, plays, short stories, articles, essays, a musical, documentaries... all apples and oranges and bananas. It's better to ask which ones I like the least. But don't expect an answer to that either.

Q. How important was your upbringing to your writing?

Let's see, I spent my first eighteen years on the Reserve, and practically all of my dramatic work deals with being Native and to some extent dealing with life on the Reserve; and, that includes a fair amount of my non-fiction work too. Doing the math, I'd have to say fairly important. Theatre is cheaper than therapy.

Q. If you weren't a writer, what would you probably have been?

I always wanted to be an astronomer, but I heard a rumour that you had to be good at math. Since I need both an accountant and a bookkeeper, that should state the obvious. I have substituted that ambition with continuous reruns of Star Trek (all five series.) My second choice would have been a cook or chef. I love cooking and am still trying to discover the perfect hangover soup recipe.

Q. Is everything you write Native oriented?/Are you a Native writer or a writer that happens to be Native?

This is often confused with question three but in all fairness, there are many Native writers out there who don't subscribe to the philosophy the Native writers should only write about Native things. In particular, journalists. Most journalists I know want to cover the world, not just the Native world. They find that too limiting. I've debated this question for years. My answer, there is so much to be explored in the Native universe that I could write about the First Nation community for the next one hundred years and probably not even come close to exhausting the story potential. Europe is going on three thousand years of written stories and history with no sign they are running out of ideas yet.

Q. As well as write plays, do you act?

Only in single bars.

Q. Who's your favorite writer? Who do you like to read?

For the longest time and for some reason, I only read books with the word "cheerleader" in the title. I have always been a reader. I know it's probably odd for a descendent of an oral tradition, but the written word has always had a special attraction for me. I was reading when reading wasn't cool. I have probably read more books than I have eaten Big Macs. And could you possibly say which was your favorite Big Mac? I thought not.

Both Trouble and Coffee are Brewing on the West Coast

While I've been busy writing this book, a tempest in a teapot has been brewing out west. Or more accurately, a tempest in a coffee pot. Where the Pacific Ocean meets the Great White North, Haida Gwaii (or better known as the Queen Charlotte Islands) was to serve as an unusual battle ground between the coffee empire Starbucks, and a lesser known Haida restaurant/coffee shop empire (if one shop can be called an empire) called HaidaBucks. It harks back to a Shakespeare reference "What's in a name?" Or perhaps better paraphrased, "Coffee served by any other name would still smell (taste) as bitter."

A small Native owned and operated organization in Massett, B.C. (population 1,200), HaidaBucks opened in 1999 as a sixty seat restaurant. Co-owner Darren Swanson describes the restaurant as having a traditional West Coast Long House facade, and offers everything from quesadillas to seafood specials. And yes, they do serve coffee, though one wonders if the fact its rival's coffee competitor known as Seattle's Best. Aye, "there's the rub," as Shakespeare (affectionately known to Native people as Shaking Spear) would again say.

"Seattle" by the way, is a legitimate Aboriginal name of a great Chief, famous for his "We are all strands in the web of life" speech, who probably never drank coffee.

On March 4th, 2004, Starbucks Coffee Company, reportedly sent a Cease and Desist letter to HaidaBucks requesting they stop the use of a confusing variation of the Starbucks name and trademark. According to their web site at the time, they were "required to take action against any individual or entity that is infringing our trademark rights. Trademark law does not permit us to be selective in protecting our rights; anytime there is infringement or dilution, we must 'police' our mark, regardless of the infringer's size. We actually risk damaging and possibly losing our trademark rights if we fail to do so."

HaidaBucks' co-owner Darren Swanson claimed Starbucks was barking up the wrong West Coast rain forest tree. In all the press, he maintained the "Bucks" part of his establishment's name refers to Aboriginal culture, not coffee culture. Swanson was quoted as saying, "Aboriginal men are called bucks. We're also Haidas, so HaidaBucks. That's how we came up with the name. Lots of men out here are called

141

Haida bucks. It's kind of our pet name."

In actuality, the term "buck" is often used as a pejorative term for adult males across North America. The Delaware Reserve, Moraviantown, near Chatham is colloquially referred to as Bucktown. Though not an expert, I also believe "buck" is a term used in this same context in the Black community.

Swanson insisted that the name of his establishment reflects that fact that it is owned and operated by four Haida guys (they even had a basketball team when they were younger named The Bucks) and they had no intention, or desire to align themselves with Starbucks. Ironically, Starbucks took its own name from a character in the Herman Melville novel Moby Dick, a book which has long since passed into public domain.

Since Canadians love a good underdog, HaidaBucks was inundated with public support. They set up a web site to cater to the 100,000 plus visitors they expected to log onto the site for more information (www.haidabuckscafe.com.) It was enough to make Starbucks blink. According to the media, the publicly traded, global conglomerate offered to give the small cafe until the end of the year to change its name and reimburse them for some of the costs associated with changing their trademark. The Aboriginal entrepreneurs countered this by staking their own claim on the term 'bucks', as one that was used in Native cultures even before Starbucks existed. They also let the media know that Joseph Arvay, a lawyer with Arvay and Finlay Barristers, had offered to represent them. HaidaBucks had pulled out the major guns because Mr. Arvay is no stranger to representing Canada's Indigenous peoples. He represented Delgamuukw before the Supreme Court of Canada and now serves counsel for the Haida Nation in their Aboriginal title claim.

David versus Goliath? White corporate America versus a small Aboriginal business? Last time I checked, the HaidaBucks web site and all traces of its existence had disappeared, except for one lonely web page I found doing a general search on the HaidaBucks name. That unidentified web page said that Starbucks, might Goliath, had backed down and was no longer interested in pursuing its claim against HaidaBucks. So I guess when it comes to this 'brew' haha, what they say is true... size doesn't matter.

FILE THIS UNDER ESCARGOT AND STEAK TARTAR

Occasionally I get asked by some poor fool who actually thinks I might know something, whether I can boil down or synthesize, as briefly as possible, the essential differences between Native people and white people into one simple example. Many wise and learned men have spent their careers researching and debating that very topic. Surprisingly, I think I have found one such example; and, it was lurking in my morning cup of coffee all this time.

Coffee beans are grown all around the world and the final product comes in many different flavours and prices. An average, good quality brand will usually set you back about $12 a pound. For many, it is manna from heaven and a day without coffee is not a day worth living. One of the more expensive brands of black liquid is called Blue Mountain, which comes from the fertile hills of Jamaica and cost; $75 a pound for that morning jolt. I've always thought coffee was a pretty expensive addiction since glass for glass it is substantially more expensive than most beer and wines.

Recently, it has come to light of an even more expensive brand of coffee on the market. One so expensive that there are only four stores in Canada that carry it. Kopi Luwak costs $600 a pound! Heroin's a cheaper high. Now that in itself is marginally interesting, but doesn't necessarily answer our philosophical questions as to the true nature of Aboriginal/Caucasian differences. That comes via the way the coffee is harvested.

In a far away land called Indonesia, is an island called Sumatra. They grow and sell a lot of coffee beans there. Some of the best in the world, in fact. On that island is an animal that likes coffee almost as much as we do. It's a marsupial, from the same family as possums and kangaroos, called Paradoxure. Paradoxure loves raw coffee beans. The raw beans are too hard for humans to digest. But Paradoxures can eat them, and they eat a lot of them, and eventually, nature and a good digestive system takes its course. So, believe it or not, the local Natives scour the jungle forests to collect *processed and discarded* coffee beans. They sell them to local coffee brokers who promptly package the (hopefully) freshly washed beans and send them to places like North America where people will pay a fortune for a coffee prized for it's earthy flavour (a unique way of phrasing it). $600 for a pound

143

for Marsupial droppings. And the stuff sells. Who buys almost all of it? I don't think it's a giant leap to say that, more than likely, it is White people who buy it.

I can't help wondering if the Sumatran Natives who gather this stuff were snickering to themselves and shaking their head in amazement when they came up with this idea. The idea that out there in the world White people would (basically) pay a month's rent to grind "preprocessed beans", perk them and drink it? "Good joke, huh," they probably said to one and other snickering. Another part of me wonders if this didn't start off as some big elaborate joke by the local tribes and somehow, the joke backfired. The Natives probably get a couple of bucks per pound for the beans. Enough to buy some soap and water to wash their hands, but the coffee brokers sell it for $600 a pound in Canada.

I realize I am being pan-Indian when I say I don't know many Native/Aboriginal/First Nations/Inuit persons who are so desperate for their morning fix they would willingly pay $600 for a few coffee beans. Considering the current economic state of most Native communities and individuals, it's unlikely they're part of the prime target demographic envisioned by the marketers. No doubt, the vast majority of our community would find the whole idea rather icky. Anyone who will eat garlic buttered snails would probably have no problem with coffee produced in such a manner.

I come from a community where my mother lives and breathes by her instant coffee. She once gave me a lecture because I got a $50 dollar haircut. She's a fairly good barometer on the state of the Indigenous mind, what we prefer, and what we can afford.

However, the entrepreneur in me wonders if maybe we can tap into this whole possum poop thing and use it for some sort of economic development in our own communities. Assembly of First Nations and Indian and Northern Development –pay attention. In central Ontario there's a reserve called Wahta (formally Gibson's), which has a reputation for harvesting a sizable crop of cranberries every year. It's a large and successful industry. I wonder what would happen if they ran a few cranberries through some of the local raccoons. It might up the profits a bit. Raccoon flavoured cranberries... could be the start of a new trend.

I wouldn't buy it but I bet some people would.

MR. M. EMAIL RESPONSE

Writing articles and having them published in a variety of newspapers and magazines can lead to some very interesting responses. Of course, the very nature of what I do –publish my opinion on a variety of controversial subject matter–can lead to heated discussions, at times to strong disagreements. This is part of the fun. How boring my job would be if everyone agreed with me.

Every once in a while, I get a unique response to something I've written. A response that requires further exploration. In my third book in the *Funny* series and in the Assembly of First Nations paper The Messenger, I published an article on our recent (well... within the last ten or fifteen years) Aboriginal obsession with golf. Growing up, no one I knew played the game. Today, everybody I know plays the game. Yet, golf has never appealed to me. I had mentioned in the article that many of the top Native actors in Canada had cut their hair and how both were a symbol of the changing face of our Native people. Someone took exception to my puzzlement at the popularity of golf and responded.

So in all fairness, I am sharing that email, along with my response.

I have just completed reading your article in the January/February issue of the First Nations Messenger and am quite astonished at your comments. Why wouldn't you ever take up the game of golf? You afraid you might not be able to hit that small white ball? Probably... because it takes skill to hit it straight. What do you suggest we Natives take up as a sport? Should we go back to Bingo or better yet, go back to alcohol? Maybe you are trying to hang on to your alcoholism and Bingo but for a Native like myself, no thanks, I'll stick with golf, and hockey, and snowmobiling and exercising and sportsmanship. You know, I don't understand why a newspaper would print idiocy like what is coming from your computer. Yes I know about the incident with the graveyard at Oka that was turned into a golf course and I was very angry about that... but the golf courses I play on are not on graveyards. If you want the Aboriginal feminist aspect on this you

would be surprised to know that thousands of Native women have also discovered this sport that promotes sportsmanship. Maybe you should try it Taylor. You know you sound like a person who dislikes sports because of your idiotic comments. By the way, what's wrong with Cricket? Don't tell me you can't hit a bigger ball with a flat stick either. I'm very interested to read your email back to me. And... I hope that you do answer your emails... if you don't what's the use of having email if you don't answer. From: A golfer and Native at that.
Mr. M.

p.s. I have short hair too! You know the next page in the paper where your sad article was, had a huge write up on an aboriginal golfer.

I responded:

Dear Mr. M.,
I read your email (as you can tell I do return my emails) and was quite surprised at the strength of your response. But that is the price of individuality, very few people have the same opinion. I'm glad you have a sport to embrace. I work out at the gym, bike, run, my little bit to combat the sedentary lifestyle writers have. I have a history of diabetes in my family so I am constantly on guard.

I, by no means, meant any disrespect to any golfers who read the article. I believe the technical term for what I wrote is called, and forgive me if the description is a bit complicated, "a joke." I was hired by The Messenger to provide (hopefully) humorous observations on Aboriginal life. I have noticed an increased predilection for the game, far more now then in my childhood, and I reported on it with a tongue-in-cheek perspective. The assertions I made in the column have been made said to my golfing friends who laughed and agreed that the game takes up far too much of their time and money. But they love the game anyway. I find that funny. I'm sorry if you don't.

Contrary to your accusations, I haven't played bingo since I was a kid (and that was only three times) and to the best of my knowledge

I am not an alcoholic, (but I do admit to having a glass of wine yesterday.)

I'm sorry if the piece angered you but I'll let you in on a secret... it wasn't meant to be taken seriously. The style and tone of the article was satiric observation, not objective journalism. People who read my work may not agree with my written comments but will often appreciate the different perspective I occasionally provide. I assure you I am not that phobic about golf; I couldn't care less about the game. As Mark Twain said, "A game of golf is a good walk spoiled."

I appreciate your response, however serious the tone, and hope any offense I may have caused you has been explained.

Drew Hayden Taylor

p.s. If it's any consolation, I too have short hair and always have had.

Buffalo Tracks

Gary Farmer once hired me to write some opening monologues for a talk show he produced called *Buffalo Tracks*. That's not my natural forte but having a hungry landlord, I gave it a shot and did a few. What follows is one of the best, and it ties into host Lucy Idlout's culture. Doing the writer thing, I tried to put myself into her mind to talk about what might be fun and interesting for her while working on a television show way down here in Toronto so far from her home of Nunavut. It turned out kind of silly, but most monologues are.

Welcome to Buffalo Tracks. I'm your host, Lucy Idlout and I'm pretty excited because.... I don't know if you've heard but evidently word on the street says being Inuit is in! Really in. Ever since *Atanarjuat: The Fast Runne*r came out, being Inuit is the cool thing to be. The film is sort of like our *Dances With Wolves*. Now way up North, we all knew being Inuit was cool... no pun intended... and we figured if we waited long enough the rest of the world would realize it too. But it sure took you guys long enough to click in.

For instance, I bet you can't go a day without seeing an inukshuk somewhere. Trent University in Peterborough has one right out front. They're on our coins. Heck, you can even get a pocket sized inukshuk for a couple bucks in a tourist shop. On top of that, now we've got German groupies coming to all our seal hunts. And there's talk of the CBC shooting a new series up in Nunavut called *Hudson's Baywatch*.

And it just gets more ridiculous. One of our writers said that last summer in Georgian Bay, he went out sea-kayaking with some friends. The operative word here being *kayaking*, one of our most favorite and ancient means of transportation. But he was confused by what he saw. There were sixteen people on that trip. As they were getting into their kayaks, he looked long and deep into their eyes and souls. And do you know what he discovered? None of them were Inuit! What's up with that?

Sixteen people kayaking –one Ojibway, fifteen White people, no Inuit. Now that's what I call some serious cultural appropriation.It's one of the drawbacks of being in, of being cool. I guess everybody wants to be you... or paddle like you anyway.

Don't get me wrong. It's not all bad. In fact, because of all this popularity the rest of the world is going to get a chance to taste some of our down home cooking. That's right. Some northern delicacies are going to make it to a fast food joint near you –if you're lucky. Have you ever heard of muktuk? Well, what it is, is raw whale meat in particular the skin and blubber beneath it. Tasty, huh? Word has it that MacDonald's is interested in marketing muktuk world wide! I kid you not. Except they want to call it McMuktuk. And I'll be first in line! And I bet you Herbie will be right with me, won't you Herbie? Do you want your order with or without fries?

Welcome to the show everybody and let's have some fun."

Note: If sometime in the far future someone decides to do an Aboriginal Trivial Pursuit game, here's a tidbit of information under the TV section. My name was misspelled in the opening six shows and APTN refused to correct it. See if you can find them.

Outkast are Outcasts in the Native Community

The wagons are circled and the Natives are restless for sure. Emails and condemnations are flying across North America quicker then broken treaty promises. For the second time in as many months, a major American television musical spectacle, this time the Grammy's instead of the Super Bowl halftime show, has provoked an outcry. Only this time, Janet Jackson's nipple was nowhere in sight. Instead, it was the performance by rap artists Outkast of their hit song, "Hey ya" that has the Native community of both America and Canada on the war path.

Near the end of the show on February 8th, 2004, the band took to the stage, emerging from a fake bright green teepee, and proceeded to bump and grind with their back-up dancers, barely scantily clad in feathered pseudo-head-dresses, fringe skirts and hotpants, and braided wigs. The University of Southern California band later joined them onstage also wearing war paint and feathered head-dresses in what many Aboriginal viewers called totally inappropriate and insulting.

It was the most disgusting set of racial stereotypes aimed at American Indians that I have ever seen on TV, said Sean Freitas, (a board member of the Native American Culture Centre –NACC), who felt it was on par with white people dancing sexually in black face. As a result, the NACC (located in San Francisco) is calling on CBS to issue a formal apology to the viewing nation. And it's not just American Indians that have found fault with the Grammy telecast. Ojibway Poet Kateri Akiwenzie-Damm found that the performance was staged and choreographed in a way that was perhaps the most tiresome, vacuous, and most disrespectful exploitation of Native American culture seen in years. It's time for the appropriation, exploitation and desecration of Aboriginal culture to stop! This is not just an American Indian issue, but should be of concern to all thoughtful, caring, honest people.

In an email sent to various Native Listserves, Penny Gummerson, Native Canadian author of the play *Wawatay* referred to the musical number as a rather tasteless performance... their use of Native American props and clothing was rather appalling. She included her voice in the growing demand, sponsored by the NACC, for an international boycott of CBS, OutKast's label Arista Records, and the

National Academy of Recording Artists And Science (who sponsored the awards). Gummerson added, Native people have long been forced to accept our subservient role in Canadian/American society. This has to stop, we can no longer accept false and offensive behaviour such as this.

Well known Native arts coordinator and producer of the popular Toronto Real Rez Bluez concert series Elaine Bomberry was in the audience that night, she said watching Outkast's performance was a truly painful experience that cut very deep... after all these years we're still presented in a such a stereotypical, horrific way. What was even sadder was that everyone was on their feet cheering, screaming, completely oblivious to the racial spectacle they just witnessed. It went right over their heads. We were surrounded.

Andrew Brother Elk, Chairman of the NACC has also lodged a complaint with the American Federal Communications Commission, saying he found the performance racist saying, if people were wearing yarmulkes and Hasidic dress were bumping and grinding, we would see that as ridiculous, but for some reason we don't see what OutKast did as ridiculous. Another Native organization, Indianz.com, launched an online petition calling for an apology from the group. Last I heard, there were over 2,500 signatures on the petition.

What particularly irked many Native viewers was the rampant disrespect of traditional Native symbols and items. Brother Elk cited the use of feathers, sacred symbols of Native Americans, as a particular abuse. Akiwenzie-Damm said it was her understanding is they also used a ceremonial "Beauty Way" song without permission from the Navajo Nation and in an utterly inappropriate way.

The NACC's call for a boycott has resulted with a flood of over 1,000 emails in support from across the United States and Canada. Radio stations from Alaska to Florida have picked up on the story and are talking about racism in the media. Indigenous communities across North America have joined the NACC in strongly protesting the circumstances surrounding the OutKast Grammy appearance. A CBS spokeswoman Nancy Cann, in response to the growing outcry, is reported to have offered apologies "if anyone was offended" by the CBS broadcast.

Not good enough, feels Andrew Brother Elk, who said there has been no formal response from CBS. It was just a comment reported in a paper. Second, an actual apology when it comes should be from Les Moonvies, head of CBS, and specifically address the outrageous racism CBS broadcast into millions of homes on Sunday. (They) need to explain to the country how this could have gotten on the air in the first place without someone saying "gee, this is offensive racism, it is not entertainment.

Brother Elk stated in a press release that even with an apology, the NACC would continue to press for an FCC investigation of the TV incident, and if it appears that the offending parties knowingly broadcast racism, that NACC would demand penalties.

Elaine Bomberry perhaps put it best when she said so much work behind the scenes by Indigenous people all over Turtle Island over many years has gone on to ensure that racial stereotypes about Indigenous peoples are not reinforced, then one production number on the Grammys throws us back many years. Together we can demand a public apology.

Granted, the topic is a dicey one. As a writer, I've frequently used symbols, metaphors, even language from other cultures in this world to illustrate what ever point I was dealing with in my writing. It's a case by case situation, where you evaluate what you are trying to achieve, and by what manner. Every artist at some point does this because there are no set law or rules. At the Calgary Stampede, you will see thousands of Indians dressed up as cowboys. Sometimes acting ridiculous, and I've yet to hear an outcry from any Cowboys Anti-Defamation league. We're all familiar with actors of various cultures playing Native roles on television and film. But I've seen Native actors playing plenty of non-Native roles: Afghan traders, Central American soldiers, Japanese characters, Filipino mothers... and some not very well. Are Native people doing a disservice to those people. Native people drinking green beer on St. Patrick's Day or doing martial arts exhibits also comes to mind.

At one First Nations conference, I saw an evening of Aboriginal entertainment that ran the spectrum of fabulous to shocking, including one dance routine by a group from Quebec, choreographed in the most stereotypical manner one could imagine. Picture a dozen or so female dancers, in buckskin dresses, waving their arms in the air like grass in the wind, and literally doing a Hollywood tom-tom dance, with arms moving in a piston-like manner as they danced around in a circle. I along with the vast majority of the audience, sat with our mouths open, in shock. We couldn't believe this was a self-choreographed Native troupe. I'm sure it out-tackyed what was seen on the Grammys.

If anybody cares, OutKast won three Grammys that night, including Album of the Year for Speakerboxx/The Love Below. The duo is up for six awards at next month's 35th Annual NAACP Image Awards, though the Native American Cultural Center is calling on the NAACP, in support, to reconsider the band's nominations. It will be interesting to see their response.

And yet, lead singer of OutKast, Andre "3000" Benjamin showed both nipples. My, how things can change in a month.

CONCLUSION

Well, Boys and girls. That's it. *Adios. Ch'meegwetch.* Ta ta.

By "it" I mean *Funny, You Don't Look Like One –Four.* I'm sorry to say this is the last of the *Funny, You Don't Look Like One* adventures. It's been four fabulous editions and four fabulous excuses to have a book launch.

When I started putting these books together back in the mid 1990s, I never envisioned coming out with a *Funny –Four*, let alone the possibility of a *Funny, You Don't Look Like One –Seventy-Eight.* Let's face it, it might get kind of redundant after a while. So get out while the gettin's good, as they say. Oh, I doubt I'll stop writing my ramblings or silly ponderings about my fun excursions, but for now, I think I've said enough as a Blue-eyed Ojibway. There are many other incarnations worth exploring.

But before the curtain closes, a hearty thank you to you all for hanging around this long. We've had a few laughs, talked about some interesting things, all the stuff good friends should do. Maybe we'll meet again over coffee or a beer. Or a "coffeer" Till then, it has been a pleasure sharing thoughts with you and I hope you have many futile and furious adventures of your own. If not, give me a call, I think I might be able to arrange something.

...don't forget to turn out the lights when you leave.